lonely planet

KT-415-689

Pocket
AMSTERDAM

TOP SIGHTS • LOCAL LIFE • MADE EASY

Catherine Le Nevez, Abigail Blasi

In This Book

QuickStart Guide

Your keys to understanding the city – we help you decide what to do and how to do it

Need to Know
Tips for a smooth trip

Neighbourhoods
What's where

Explore Amsterdam

The best things to see and do, neighbourhood by neighbourhood

Top Sights
Make the most of your visit

Local Life
The insider's city

The Best of Amsterdam

The city's highlights in handy lists to help you plan

Best Walks
See the city on foot

Amsterdam's Best...
The best experiences

Survival Guide

Tips and tricks for a seamless, hassle-free city experience

Getting Around
Travel like a local

Essential Information
Including where to stay

Our selection of the city's best places to eat, drink and experience:

⊙ **Sights**

✖ **Eating**

🅐 **Drinking**

✪ **Entertainment**

🔒 **Shopping**

These symbols give you the vital information for each listing:

☎	Telephone Numbers	👨‍👩‍👧	Family-Friendly
☺	Opening Hours	🐾	Pet-Friendly
P	Parking	🚌	Bus
🚭	Nonsmoking	🚢	Ferry
@	Internet Access	M	Metro
🛜	Wi-Fi Access	S	Subway
🌱	Vegetarian Selection	⊖	London Tube
📖	English-Language Menu	🚋	Tram
		🚆	Train

Find each listing quickly on maps for each neighbourhood:

Bar Hemingway

16 🅐 Map p233, B2

Legend has it that Hemi
self, wielding a machine
rate this timber-pan
ered bar during
showpiece is a
en by Papa ar
town. Dress
s.com; Hôtel Rit
; ☺6.30pm-2a

QuickStart Guide 7

Explore Amsterdam 21

Worth a Trip:

The Best of Amsterdam 151

Amsterdam's Best Walks

Amsterdam's Best...

Survival Guide 173

QuickStart Guide

Welcome to Amsterdam

Amsterdam showcases its Dutch heritage in its charming canal architecture, museums filled with works by Old Masters, *jenever* (Dutch gin) tasting houses and candlelit *bruin cafés* (traditional Dutch pubs). Yet this free-spirited city is also a multinational melting pot with an incredible diversity of cultures and cuisines, along with some of Europe's hottest nightlife venues, in a compact, village-like setting.

Dutch houses and houseboats on the Singel canal (p59)
KAVALENKAVA/SHUTTERSTOCK ©

Amsterdam Top Sights
Top Sights

Royal Palace (Koninklijk Paleis; p24)

Amsterdam's resplendent palace is infused with history.

Begijnhof (p26)
Historic central Amsterdam courtyard.

Anne Frank Huis (p44)

Amsterdam's most poignant history lesson.

Van Gogh Museum (p90)

World's greatest Van Gogh collection.

Rijksmuseum (p86)

Thrillingly fine national art museum.

Vondelpark (p94)

Amsterdam's best-loved, chilled-out park.

Tropenmuseum (p118)

Fascinating tropical artifacts, creatively presented.

Museum het Rembrandthuis (p128)

Rembrandt's former house and studio.

Amsterdam
Local Life

*Local experiences and hidden gems
to help you uncover the real city*

In between visiting the city's famous sights, seek out the off-beat music clubs, bohemian artist quarters, sweet patisseries and quirky local shops that make up the locals' Amsterdam. Count on *bruin cafés* (traditional pubs) and canals making appearances.

Shopping the Jordaan & Western Canal Ring (p46)

☑ Small, oddball shops ☑ *Bruin cafés*

Westerpark & Western Islands (p64)

☑ Amsterdam School architecture
☑ Edgy cultural park

INNAFELKER/SHUTTERSTOCK ©

MARK READ/LONELY PLANET ©

Strolling the Southern Canal Ring (p68)

☑Golden Age mansions ☑Swanky antique shops

Discovering Bohemian De Pijp (p106)

☑Flea market ☑Cafes in historic buildings

Café-Hopping in Nieuwmarkt & Plantage

(p130)☑Amsterdam's biggest market ☑Hip bars

Amsterdam Day Planner

Day One

☀ Begin with the biggies: tram to the Museum Quarter to ogle the masterpieces at the **Van Gogh Museum** (p90) and **Rijksmuseum** (p86). They'll be crowded, so make sure you've prebooked tickets. Modern-art buffs might want to swap the **Stedelijk Museum** (p97) for one of the others.

☀ Spend the afternoon in the Medieval Centre. Explore the secret courtyard and gardens at the **Begijnhof** (p26). Walk up the street to the **Dam** (p31), where the **Royal Palace** (p24) and **Nieuwe Kerk** (p30) provide a dose of Dutch history. Bend over to sip your *jenever* (Dutch gin) like a local at **Wynand Fockink** (p36).

☽ Venture into the Red Light District for an eye-popping array of fetish-gear shops, live sex shows, smoky coffee-shops and, of course, women in day-glo lingerie beckoning from crimson windows. Then settle in to a *bruin café* (traditional Dutch pub), such as **In 't Aepjen** (p35).

Day Two

☀ Browse the **Albert Cuypmarkt** (p106), Amsterdam's largest street bazaar, an international free-for-all of cheeses, fish, *stroopwafels* (syrup-filled waffles) and bargain-priced clothing. Then submit to the **Heineken Experience** (p109) to get shaken up, heated up and 'bottled' like the beer you'll drink at the end of the brewery tour.

☀ Cross into the Southern Canal Ring and stroll along the grand Golden Bend. Visit **Museum Van Loon** (p72) for a peek into the opulent canal-house lifestyle, or get a dose of kitty quirk at the **Kattenkabinet** (p69). Browse the **Bloemenmarkt** (p68) and behold the wild array of bulbs.

☽ When the sun sets, it's time to par-tee at hyperactive, neon-lit Leidseplein. **Paradiso** (p81) and **Melkweg** (p81) host the coolest agendas. Otherwise the good-time clubs and *bruin cafés* (traditional Dutch pubs) around the square beckon.

Short on time?
We've arranged Amsterdam's must-sees into these day-by-day itineraries to make
sure you see the very best of the city in the time you have available.

Day Three

☀ Take a spin around beloved **Von-delpark** (p94). Long and narrow (about 1.5km long and 300m wide), it's easy to explore via a morning jaunt. All the better if you have a bicycle to zip by the ponds, gardens and sculptures.

☀ Immerse yourself in the **Negen Straatjes** (p47) (Nine Streets), a tic-tac-toe board of speciality shops. The **Anne Frank Huis** (p44) is also in the neighbourhood, and it's a must. The claustrophobic rooms, their windows still covered with blackout screens, give an all-too-real feel for Anne's life in hiding. Seeing the diary itself – filled with her sunny writing tempered with quiet despair – is moving, plain and simple.

☾ Dine with a canal view at **De Belhamel** (p53), then spend the evening in the Jordaan, the chummy district embodying the Amsterdam of yore. Hoist a glass on a canal-side terrace at **'t Smalle** (p55), join the houseboat party at **Café P 96** (p58), or quaff beers at one of the many *gezellig* (cosy) haunts.

Day Four

☀ Mosey through **Waterlooplein Flea Market** (p131) in Nieuwmarkt. Rembrandt sure loved markets, if his nearby studio is any indication. **Museum het Rembrandthuis** (p128) gives a peek at the master's inner sanctum. Neighbouring **Gassan Diamonds** (p136) gives free tours. Or check out the intriguing **Verzetsmuseum** (p135), the Resistance Museum, or sea treasures at **Het Scheepvaartmuseum** (p134).

☀ Hop on a free ferry to Noord, one of the city's coolest, most up-and-coming neighbourhoods. Check out the cinematic exhibits at the **EYE Film Institute** (p146) and the artists' studios in the sprawling **Kunststad** (Art City; p146) centre at former shipyards **NDSM-werf** (p145). Ascend **A'DAM Tower** (p145) for dazzling views across the IJ River to the city centre.

☾ There are some fantastic nightlife venues in Noord; alternatively, back on the city side of the IJ, an evening spent on the terrace at **De Ysbreeker** (p124), looking out over the bustling, houseboat-strewn Amstel River, is a well-deserved treat.

Need to Know

For more information,
see Survival Guide (p174)

Currency
Euro (€)

Language
Dutch

Visas
Generally not required for stays of up to three months. Some nationalities require a Schengen visa.

Money
ATMs widely available. Credit cards accepted in most hotels but not all restaurants. Non-European credit cards are sometimes rejected.

Mobile Phones
Beware of high roaming charges from non-EU countries. Local prepaid SIM cards are widely available and can be used in most unlocked phones.

Time
Central European Time (GMT/UTC plus one hour)

Tipping
Leave 5% to 10% for a cafe snack (or round up to the next euro), 10% or so for a restaurant meal. Tip taxi drivers 5% to 10%.

❶ Before You Go

Your Daily Budget

Budget: Less than €100
▶ Dorm bed: €25–60
▶ Supermarkets and lunchtime specials for food: €20

Midrange: €100–250
▶ Double room: €150
▶ Three-course dinner in casual restaurant: €35
▶ Canal Bus day pass: €21

Top end: More than €250
▶ Four-star hotel double room: from €250
▶ Five-course dinner in top restaurant: from €80
▶ Private canal-boat rental for two hours: from €90

Useful Websites

Lonely Planet (www.lonelyplanet.com/amsterdam) Destination information, hotel bookings, traveller forum and more.

I Amsterdam (www.iamsterdam.com) City-run portal.

Dutch News (www.dutchnews.nl) News and event listings.

Advance Planning

Four months before Book your accommodation, especially if you're visiting in summer or on a weekend.

Two months before Check club and performing arts calendars and buy tickets.

Two weeks before Make dinner reservations at your must-eat restaurants, reserve walking or cycling tours, and purchase tickets online to popular attractions.

② Arriving in Amsterdam

Most people flying to Amsterdam arrive at Schiphol International Airport (AMS; www.schiphol.nl), 18km southwest of the city centre. National and international trains arrive at Centraal Train Station in the city centre.

✈ From Schiphol International Airport

Train Trains run to Amsterdam's Centraal Station (€5.20 one way, 15 minutes) 24 hours a day. From 6am to 12.30am they go every 10 minutes or so; hourly in the wee hours. The rail platform is inside the terminal, down the escalator.

Shuttle bus A shuttle van is run by Connexxion (www.schipholhotelshuttle.nl; one way/return €17/27), every 30 minutes from 7am to 9pm, from the airport to several hotels. Look for the Connexxion desk by Arrivals 4.

Bus Bus 197/Amsterdam Airport Express (€5 one way, 25 minutes) is the quickest way to places by the Museumplein, Leidseplein or Vondelpark. It departs outside the arrivals hall door. Buy a ticket from the driver.

Taxi Taxis take 20 to 30 minutes to the centre (longer in heavy traffic), costing around €37.50. The taxi stand is just outside the arrivals hall door.

🚉 From Centraal Train Station

Tram Of Amsterdam's 15 tram lines, 10 stop at Centraal Station, and then fan out to the rest of the city. For trams 4, 9, 16, 24 and 26, head far to the left (east) when you come out the station's main entrance; look for the 'A' sign. For trams 1, 2, 5, 13 and 17, head to the right (west) and look for the 'B' sign.

Taxi Taxis queue near the front station entrance toward the west side. Fares are meter-based. It should be €15 to €20 for destinations in the centre, canal ring or Jordaan.

③ Getting Around

GVB passes in chip-card form are the most convenient option for public transport. Buy them at GVB ticket offices or visitor centres. Tickets aren't sold on board. Always wave your card at the pink machine when entering and departing.

🏃 Walking

Central Amsterdam is compact and very easy to cover by foot.

🚲 Bicycle

This is the locals' main mode of getting around. Rental companies are all over town; bikes cost about €12 per day.

🚊 Tram

Fast, frequent and ubiquitous, operating between 6am and 12.30am.

🚌 Bus & Metro

Primarily serve the outer districts; not much use in the city centre.

⛴ Ferry

Free ferries depart for Amsterdam Noord from docks behind Centraal Station.

🚗 Taxi

Expensive and often slow due to Amsterdam's narrow, canal-woven streets.

Amsterdam Neighbourhoods

Worth a Trip
◯ Local Life
Westerpark & Western Islands (p64)

Medieval Centre & Red Light District (p22)
Amsterdam's medieval core mixes fairy-tale Golden Age buildings, *bruin cafés* and the lurid Red Light District.

◉ Top Sights
Royal Palace (Koninklijk Paleis)
Begijnhof

Jordaan & the Western Canal Ring (p42)
The Jordaan teems with cosy pubs and lanes ideal for getting lost. The Western Canal Ring unfurls quirky boutiques and waterside *cafés*.

◉ Top Sight
Anne Frank Huis

Vondelpark & the South (p84)
Vondelpark is a green lung with personality, adjacent to the genteel Old South, home to Amsterdam's grandest museums.

◉ Top Sights
Rijksmuseum
Van Gogh Museum
Vondelpark

Southern Canal Ring (p66)
By day, visit the city's less-heralded museums. By night, party at the clubs around Leidseplein and Rembrandtplein.

Anne Frank Huis ◉

Royal Palace ◉
(Koninklijk Paleis)

Begijnhof ◉

Vondelpark ◉
Rijksmuseum ◉
Van Gogh Museum ◉

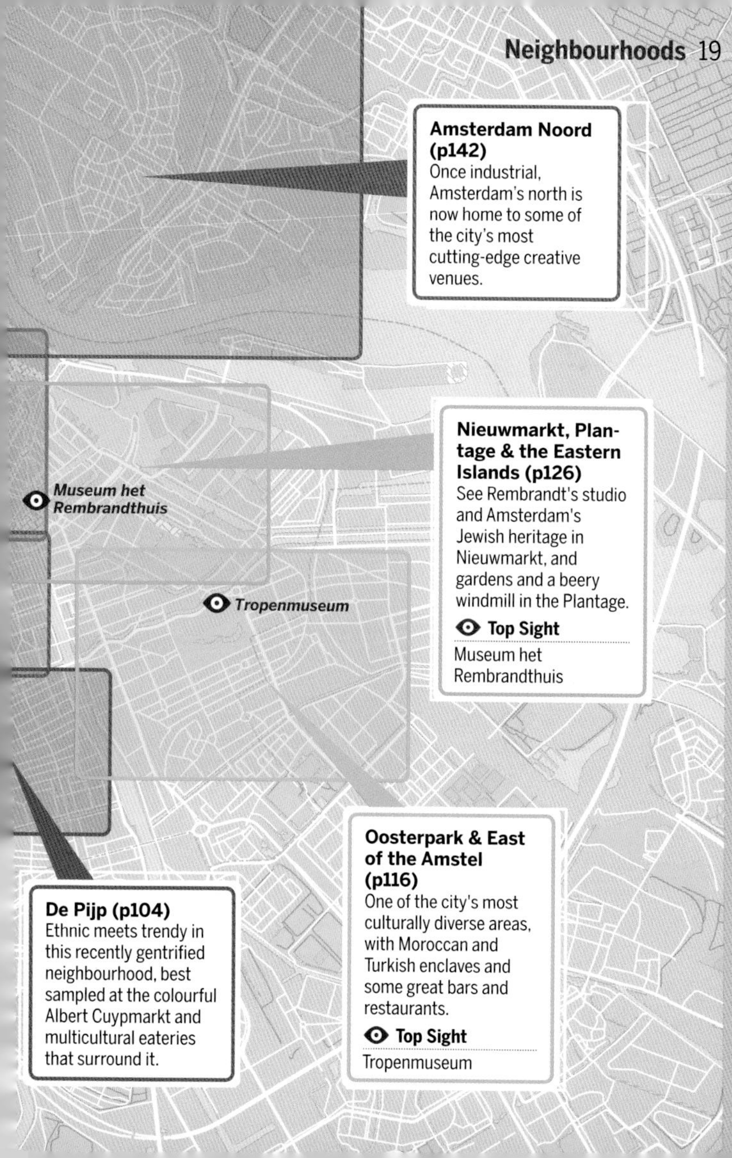

Amsterdam Noord (p142)
Once industrial, Amsterdam's north is now home to some of the city's most cutting-edge creative venues.

Nieuwmarkt, Plantage & the Eastern Islands (p126)
See Rembrandt's studio and Amsterdam's Jewish heritage in Nieuwmarkt, and gardens and a beery windmill in the Plantage.

⊙ Top Sight

Museum het Rembrandthuis

⊙ *Museum het Rembrandthuis*

⊙ *Tropenmuseum*

Oosterpark & East of the Amstel (p116)
One of the city's most culturally diverse areas, with Moroccan and Turkish enclaves and some great bars and restaurants.

⊙ Top Sight

Tropenmuseum

De Pijp (p104)
Ethnic meets trendy in this recently gentrified neighbourhood, best sampled at the colourful Albert Cuypmarkt and multicultural eateries that surround it.

Explore
Amsterdam

Worth a Trip

Houses on the Brouwersgracht canal (p59)
CARLOS S. PEREYRA/AGE FOTOSTOCK ©

Explore

Medieval Centre & Red Light District

Amsterdam's oldest quarter is remarkably preserved, looking much as it did in its Golden Age heyday. It's the busiest part of town for visitors. While some come to see the Royal Palace and Oude Kerk, others make a beeline for the coffeeshops and Red Light District.

JORG GREUEL/GETTY IMAGES ©

The Sights in a Day

☀️ Look for the secret courtyard at the **Begijnhof** (p26), which is at its most serene early morning. Pop into the **Amsterdam Museum** (p30) to learn local history, then see it in person at the Dam, where the city was founded. The 15th-century **Nieuwe Kerk** (p30) and 17th-century **Royal Palace** (p24; pictured left) also huddle here.

☀️ Grab lunch at **Gartine** (p33) and venture into the Red Light District. There's more here than you might think. The 700-year-old **Oude Kerk** (p30) has a who's who of famous folks buried beneath its floor, while **Museum Ons' Lieve Heer op Solder** (p30) hides a relic-rich church behind its canal-house facade. You can see titillating stuff too: walk down Warmoesstraat or Oudezijds Achterburgwal, past **Mr B** (p41) and **Casa Rosso** (p39).

🌙 Feast cheaply at **Chinatown** (p33) or dine on contemporary Dutch dishes at **Lt Cornelis** (p34). Belly up to the bar for a Dutch *jenever* (gin) at **Wynand Fockink** (p36) or **In de Olofspoort** (p36). Or sip at **Hoppe** (p37) on the *café*-ringed Spui.

👁 Top Sights

Royal Palace (Koninklijk Paleis; p24)

Begijnhof (p26)

💜 Best of Amsterdam

Best Eating

D'Vijff Vlieghen (p33)

Vleminckx (p33)

Lt Cornelis (p34)

Gartine (p33)

Best Drinking & Nightlife

In 't Aepjen (p35)

Wynand Fockink (p36)

In de Olofspoort (p36)

Tales & Spirits (p35)

Dum Dum Palace (p36)

Dampkring (p34)

Abraxas (p34)

Getting There

🚋 **Tram** Trams 1, 2, 5, 13 and 17 travel to the station's west side; trams 4, 9, 16 and 24 travel to the east side.

Ⓜ **Metro** Metros travel from Centraal to Amsterdam's outer neighbourhoods and, as of mid-2018, to Amsterdam Noord and Station Zuid, with a stop in the Medieval Centre at Rokin.

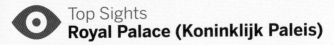

Top Sights
Royal Palace (Koninklijk Paleis)

Today's Royal Palace began life as a glorified town hall and was completed in 1665. Its architect, Jacob van Campen, spared no expense to display Amsterdam's wealth in a way that rivalled the grandest European buildings of the day. The result is opulence on a big scale. It's worth seeing the exterior at night, when the palace is dramatically floodlit.

Koninklijk Paleis

◉ Map p28, B5

☎ 020-522 61 61

www.paleisamsterdam.nl

adult/child €10/free

🕙 10am–5pm

🚊 4/9/16/24 Dam

A King's Residence

Officially the Dutch king, King Willem-Alexander, lives in this landmark palace and pays a symbolic rent, though his actual residence is in Den Haag. If he's not here in Amsterdam, visitors have the opportunity to come in and wander around the monumental building.

The 1st Floor

Most of the rooms spread over the 1st floor, which is awash in chandeliers (51 shiners in total), along with damasks, gilded clocks, and some spectacular paintings by artists including Ferdinand Bol and Jacob de Wit. The great *burgerzaal* (citizens' hall) that occupies the heart of the building was envisioned as a schematic of the world, with Amsterdam as its centre. Check out the maps inlaid in the floor; they show the eastern and western hemispheres, with a 1654 celestial map in the middle.

Empire-style Decor

In 1808 the building became the palace of King Louis, Napoleon Bonaparte's brother. In a classic slip-up in the new lingo, French-born Louis told his subjects here that he was the 'rabbit (*konijn*) of Holland', when he actually meant 'king' (*konink* – an old spelling variation of *koning*, the Dutch word for king). Napoleon dismissed him two years later. Louis left behind about 1000 pieces of Empire-style furniture and decorative artworks. As a result, the palace now holds one of the world's largest collections from the period.

☑ Top Tips

▶ The Royal Palace is still used for state functions and often closes for such events, especially during April, May, November and December. The schedule is posted on the website.

▶ When you enter, be sure to pick up the free audioguide, which vividly details the palace's main features.

✕ Take a Break

Pick up traditional Dutch *stroopwafels* (caramel syrup–filled waffles) at Firma Stroop (p34).

Sip *jenever* (Dutch gin) amid gorgeous blue-and-white Delft tiles and timber panelling at De Blauwe Parade (p37).

NMBJC7/GETTY IMAGES ©

Top Sights
Begijnhof

It feels like something out of a storybook. You walk up to the unassuming door, push it open and voila – a hidden courtyard of tiny houses and gardens opens up before you. The 14th-century Begijnhof is not a secret these days, but somehow it remains a surreal oasis of peace in the city's midst.

◉ Map p28, A7

www.nicolaas-parochie.nl

admission free

⊘9am-5pm

🚋1/2/5 Spui

History

The Beguines were a Catholic order of unmarried or widowed women who lived a religious life without taking monastic vows. The Begijnhof was their convent of sorts. The last true Beguine died in 1971.

Begijnhof Kapel

One of two churches hidden in the *hof* (courtyard), the 1671 **Begijnhof Kapel** (Begijnhof 30; ⏱1-6.30pm Mon, 9am-6.30pm Tue-Fri, 9am-6pm Sat & Sun) is a 'clandestine' chapel where the Beguines were forced to worship after the Calvinists took away their Gothic church. Go through the dog-leg entrance to find marble columns, stained-glass windows and murals commemorating the Miracle of Amsterdam (in short: in 1345 the final sacrament was administered to a dying man, but he was unable to keep down the communion wafer and brought it back up. Here's the miracle part: when the vomit was thrown on the fire, the wafer would not burn. Yes, it's all depicted in wall paintings).

Engelse Kerk

The other church is known as the **Engelse Kerk** (English Church; www.ercadam.nl; Begijnhof 48; ⏱9am-5pm), built around 1392. It was eventually rented out to the local community of English and Scottish Presbyterian refugees – including the Pilgrim Fathers – and it still serves as the city's Presbyterian church. Look for pulpit panels by Piet Mondrian, in a figurative phase. Note that as this church is still in frequent use, it's sometimes closed to visitors.

Houten Huis

Look out, too, for the **Houten Huis** (Wooden House; Begijnhof 34) at No 34. It dates from around 1465, making it the oldest preserved wooden house in the Netherlands.

☑ **Top Tips**

▶ Look for a wooden door on the Spui's north side, east of the American Book Center, to find another entrance to the Begijnhof near the Houten Huis.

▶ Today, 105 single women still live in the Begijnhof. Visitors are asked to be respectful, not to eat, drink, smoke (any substance) or litter, and to keep noise to a minimum.

✕ **Take a Break**

Dine on classic Dutch dishes at quaint Tomaz (p34).

E

Binnen Bantammerstr

Geldersekade

Geldersekade

Oudezijds Kolk

Zeedijk

Zeedijk

Stormst

Kleipaez

Centraal Station
Centraal Station (west side)
Centraal Station (east side)
Centraal Station
Stations-plein

Ⓜ

VVV I Amsterdam Visitor Centre

⊙20

Brouwerij
De Prael
Museum Ons'
Lieve Heer op Solder
⊙5 ⊙1 ⊙26
21

⊙17

22 ⊙

Oudezijds Armst

Warmoesstr

Lange Niezel

Korte Niezel

Oudezijds Voorburgwal

35 ⊙

Nieuwbrugst

D

Damrak

⊙36

⊙4 Oude Kerk

Prins Hendrikkade

Open Havenfront

Hasselaerst

Martelaarsg

Nieuwendijk

Panaasst

Oudebrugst

Beursst

C

Droogbak

Stromarkt

Sexmuseum 9 ⊙

St Jacobsstr Amsterdam

Nieuwezijds armst

Kolkst

Onze Lieve Vrouwest

Beurs-plein

⊙19

Nieuwendijk

Nieuwezijds Kolk

15 ✕ Zoutst

Droogbak

Haarlemmerstr

Herenmarkt

Brouwersgr

Singel

Langestr

Herengr

B

Koggestr

27 ✿

Spuistr

Oude Nieuwstr

D van Hasseltsst

Nieuwe Nieuwstr

St Nicolaasstr

Nieuwezijds Voorburgwal

Gravenstr

Nieuwe Kerk

⊙25
14 ✕
31 ✿

Molst

Torenst

Singel

⊙18

Blauwburgwal

Lijnbaansstr

JORDAAN

Herenstr

Herengr

Bergstr

Oude Leliestr

Torensluis

Oude Leliestr

Keizersgr

A

1

2

3

4

NIEUWMARKT

Koningsstr
Keizersstr
Dijkstr
Oude schans
Oude Schans
Jodenbreestr
Waterlooplein
Stopera
Bloedstr
Nieuwmarkt
Nieuwmarkt
St Antoniesbreestr
Nieuwe Hoogstr
Zanddwarsstr
Zandstr
Zwanenburgwal
Zwanenburgwal
Koestr
Oude Hoogstr
Raamgr
Greenburgwal
Staalstr
29
7
Cannabis College
Oudezijds Achterburgwal
Rusland
Slijkstr
Kloveniersburgwal
Nieuwe Doelenstr
Amstel
Binnen Amstel
St Annenstr
33
Oudezijds Voorburgwal
St Jansstr
23
Pijlst
CENTRUM
Damstr
Pieter Jacobszstr
St Pietershalst
28
Nes
Oudezijds Voorburgwal
Grimburgwal
Binnengasthuis UvA
Oude Turfmarkt
34
Warmoesstr
Valkenstr
6
Dam
Damrak
Kalverstr
Wijde Kapelst
Enge Kapelst
Begijnensteeg
Waterst
Takst
Spui
12
Rokin
Kalverstr
Muntplein
Royal Palace
Magna Plaza
Jonge Roelenst
St Lucienst
Nieuwezijds Voorburgwal
Gedempte Begijnensloot
8
16
13
10
Voetboogstr
Heiligeweg
Handboogstr
Singel
30
Paleisstr
Spuistr
Civic Guard Gallery
Rosmar
Amsterdam Museum
2
rijnt
Begijnhof
Spui
32
24
Raadhuisstr
Singel
Singel
Spuistr
Singel
Raamst
11
Heist
Singel

N 0
0 200 m
0 0.1 miles

Sights

Museum Ons' Lieve Heer op Solder

MUSEUM

1 ⊙ Map p28, D4

Within what looks like an ordinary canal house is an entire Catholic church. Ons' Lieve Heer op Solder (Our Dear Lord in the Attic) was built in the mid-1600s in defiance of the Calvinists. Inside you'll see labyrinthine staircases, rich artworks, period decor and the soaring, two-storey church itself. (☑020-624 66 04; www.opsolder.nl; Oudezijds Voorburgwal 38; adult/child €10/5; ⊙10am-6pm Mon-Sat, 1-6pm Sun; 🚊4/9/16/24 Dam)

Amsterdam Museum

MUSEUM

2 ⊙ Map p28, A7

Entrepreneurship, free thinking, citizenship and creativity are the four cornerstones of the multimedia DNA exhibit at this riveting museum, which splits Amsterdam's millennia-old history into seven key time periods. Unlike at many of the city's museums, crowds are rare. It's reached via the arcade containing the free Civic Guard Gallery (p32) off Kalverstraat 92. (☑020-523 18 22; www.amsterdammuseum.nl; Gedempte Begijnensloot; adult/child €12.50/6.50; ⊙10am-5pm; 🚊1/2/5 Spui)

Nieuwe Kerk

CHURCH

3 ⊙ Map p28, B4

This 15th-century, late-Gothic basilica is only 'new' in relation to the Oude Kerk (Old Church; from 1306). A few monumental items dominate the otherwise spartan interior – a magnificent carved oak chancel, a bronze choir screen, a massive organ and enormous stained-glass windows. It's the site of royal investitures and weddings and is otherwise used for art exhibitions and concerts. Opening times and prices can vary depending on what's going on. An audioguide costs €2. (New Church; ☑020-638 69 09; www.nieuwekerk.nl; Dam; €8-16; ⊙10am-6pm; 🚊1/2/5/13/14/17 Dam)

Oude Kerk

CHURCH

4 ⊙ Map p28, D4

Dating from 1306, the Oude Kerk is Amsterdam's oldest surviving building. It's also an intriguing moral contradiction: a church surrounded by active Red Light District windows. Inside, check out the stunning Vater-Müller organ, the naughty 15th-century carvings on the choir stalls and famous Amsterdammers' tombstones in the floor (including Rembrandt's wife, Saskia van Uylenburgh). Regular art exhibitions take place in the church; you can also climb the **tower** (www.westertorenamsterdam.nl; tour €8; ⊙1-7pm Mon-Sat Apr-Oct) on a guided tour. Church admission is by credit/debit card only. (Old Church; ☑020-625 82 84; https://oudekerk.nl; Oudekerksplein; adult/child €10/free; ⊙10am-6pm Mon-Sat, 1-5.30pm Sun; 🚊4/9/16/24 Dam)

Brouwerij De Prael

BREWERY

5 ⊙ Map p28, D3

Brouwerij De Prael offers engaging behind-the-scenes tours of its

Dam Square

brewery. Tours depart on the hour and last 40 minutes, followed by a sample (or four). The tasting room (p36) is a great place to try more of its wares. De Prael also makes liqueurs that you can buy at the brewery's attached shop. (📞020-408 44 70; http://deprael.nl; Oudezijds Voorburgwal 30; tour with 1/4 beers €8.50/17.50; ⏲tours hourly 1-6pm Mon-Fri, 1-5pm Sat, 2-5pm Sun; 🚊1/2/4/5/9/13/16/17/24 Centraal Station)

Dam
SQUARE

6 ◉ Map p28, B5

This square is the very spot where Amsterdam was founded around 1270. Today pigeons, tourists, buskers and the occasional funfair complete with Ferris wheel take over the grounds. It's still a national gathering spot, and if there's a major speech or demonstration it's held here. (🚊4/9/16/24 Dam)

Cannabis College
CULTURAL CENTRE

7 ◉ Map p28, D5

This nonprofit centre offers tips and tricks for having a safe smoking experience and provides the low-down on local cannabis laws. There are educational displays and a library. Staff can provide maps and advice on where to find coffeeshops that sell organic weed and shops that are good for newbies. T-shirts, stickers, postcards and a few other trinkets with the logo are for sale too. (📞020-423 44 20; www.cannabiscollege.com; Oudezijds Achterburgwal 124; ⏲11am-7pm; 🚊4/9/16/24 Dam)

Civic Guard Gallery
GALLERY

8 ◉ Map p28, A6

Part of the Amsterdam Museum (p30) – consider it the free 'teaser' – this gallery fills a laneway next to the museum's entrance. It displays 15 grand posed-group portraits, from medieval guards painted during the Dutch Golden Age (à la Rembrandt's *Night Watch*) to *Modern Civic Guards*, a rendering of Anne Frank, Alfred Heineken and a joint-smoking personification of Mokum (the nickname for the city of Amsterdam). (Kalverstraat 92; admission free; ⏰10am-5pm; 🚊1/2/5 Spui)

Sexmuseum Amsterdam
MUSEUM

9 ◉ Map p28, D3

The Sexmuseum is good for a giggle. You'll find replicas of pornographic Pompeian plates, erotic 14th-century Viennese bronzes, some of the world's earliest nude photographs, an automated farting flasher in a trench coat, and a music box that plays 'Edelweiss' and purports to show a couple in flagrante delicto. It's sillier and more fun than other erotic museums in the Red Light District. Minimum age for entry is 16. (www.sexmuseumamsterdam. nl; Damrak 18; €5; ⏰9.30am-11.30pm; 🚊1/2/4/5/9/13/16/17/24 Centraal Station)

Understand

Red Light District Clean-up

Prostitution was officially legalised in the Netherlands in 2000 and an estimated 6000 people over 21 work as prostitutes and pay taxes. But the red lights of the Red Light District were around as early as the 1300s, when women carrying red lanterns met sailors near the port.

Since 2007 city officials have been reducing the number of Red Light windows in an effort to clean up the district. They claim it's not about morals but about crime: pimps, traffickers and money launderers have entered the scene and set the neighbourhood on a downward spiral. Opponents point to a growing conservatism and say the government is using crime as an excuse, because it doesn't like Amsterdam's current reputation for sin.

As the window tally has decreased, fashion studios, art galleries and trendy cafes have moved in to reclaim the deserted spaces, thanks to a program of low-cost rent and other business incentives. To date, 300 windows remain, down from 482. Scores of prostitutes and their supporters have taken to the streets to protest the closures: the concern is that closing the windows simply forces prostitutes to relocate to less safe environments. The city is now rethinking its plan to buy back many more of the windows. In the meantime, other initiatives for changing the face of the area include the introduction of festivals such as early June's Red Light Jazz Festival (www. redlightjazz.com).

Eating

Vleminckx
FAST FOOD €

10 ✕ | Map p28, B8

Frying up *frites* (fries) since 1887, Amsterdam's best *friterie* has been based at this hole-in-the-wall takeaway shack near the Spui since 1957. The standard order of perfectly cooked crispy, fluffy *frites* is smothered in mayonnaise, though its 28 sauces also include apple, green pepper, ketchup, peanut, sambal and mustard. Queues almost always stretch down the block, but they move fast. (http://vleminckx
sausmeester.nl; Voetboogstraat 33; fries €3-5, sauces €0.70; ☉noon-7pm Sun & Mon, 11am-7pm Tue, Wed, Fri & Sat, to 8pm Thu; 🚊1/2/5 Koningsplein)

D'Vijff Vlieghen
DUTCH €€€

11 ✕ | Map p28, A7

Spread across five 17th-century canal houses, the 'Five Flies' is a jewel. Old-wood dining rooms overflow with character, featuring Delft-blue tiles and original works by Rembrandt; chairs have copper plates inscribed with the names of famous guests (Walt Disney, Mick Jagger...). Exquisite dishes range from goose breast with apple, sauerkraut and smoked butter to candied haddock with liquorice sauce. (🖀020-530 40 60; http://vijffvlieghen.nl; Spuistraat 294-302; mains €23-29; ☉6-10pm; 🚊1/2/5 Spui)

Gartine
CAFE €

12 ✕ | Map p28, B7

Gartine is magical, from its covert location in an alley off busy Kalverstraat to its mismatched antique tableware and its sublime breakfast pastries, sandwiches and salads (made from produce grown in its garden plot and eggs from its chickens). The sweet-and-savoury high tea, from 2pm to 5pm, is a treat. (🖀020-320 41 32; www.gartine.nl; Taksteeg 7; dishes €6-12, high tea €17-25; ☉10am-6pm Wed-Sat; 🗷; 🚊4/9/14/16/24 Spui/Rokin)

Lt Cornelis

DUTCH €€

13 Map p28, B8

Blending Golden Age and contemporary elements, Lt Cornelis' downstairs bar crafts signature cocktails like *drop* (liquorice), caramel *stroopwafel* and apple pie with cinnamon. Upstairs, the stunning art-gallery-like dining room has framed Dutch paintings on marine-blue walls and reinvents classic recipes such as salted herring with apple and beetroot carpaccio, and lamb with white asparagus, sea vegetables and liquorice sauce. (☎020-261 48 63; Voetboogstraat 13; mains €17-23, 3-/4-/5-course menus €35/42/47, with paired wines €54/68/81; 🚊1/2/5 Spui)

Firma Stroop

BAKERY €

14 Map p28, A4

A working cash register from 1904 stands on the counter of this *stroop-wafel* specialist. Along with classic caramel-filled, wafer-thin waffles, it bakes various other twists on this quintessential Dutch treat, such as chocolate-dipped *stroopwafels* with hazelnuts, and *stroopwafels* covered in coconut flakes or icing made from fresh strawberries. There's no on-site seating, but you'll find plenty of canal-side benches nearby. (Molsteeg 11; dishes €3-5; ⏰10am-6pm; 🚊1/2/5/13/14/17 Dam)

Rob Wigboldus Vishandel

SANDWICHES €

15 Map p28, C4

A wee three-table oasis in a narrow alleyway just off the touristy Damrak, this fish shop serves excellent herring sandwiches on a choice of crusty white or brown rolls. Other sandwich fillings include smoked eel, Dutch prawns and fried whitefish. (Zoutsteeg 6; sandwiches €2-6; ⏰9am-5pm Tue-Sat; 🚊4/9/16/24 Dam)

Tomaz

DUTCH €€

16 Map p28, B7

Charming little Tomaz hides near the Begijnhof (p26) and is a fine spot for a light lunch or an informal dinner. Staples include a daily *stamppot* (potato mashed with other vegetables), veal croquettes, IJsselmeer mussels and Dutch sausages. A vegetarian special is always available. Linger for a while over a game of chess. (☎020-320 64 89; www.tomaz.nl; Begijnensteeg 6-8; mains lunch €8-17, dinner €15-33; ⏰noon-10pm; 🚊1/2/5 Spui)

☑ Top Tip

Café vs Coffeeshop

There's a *big* difference between a *café* (aka pub) and a coffeeshop, which is where one procures marijuana. Of the numerous options, **Dampkring** (Map p28, A8; http://dampkring-coffeeshop-amsterdam.nl; Handboogstraat 29; ⏰8am-1am; 📶; 🚊1/2/5 Koningsplein), with its comprehensive menu, and mellow **Abraxas** (Map p28, B6; http://abraxas.tv; Jonge Roelensteeg 12; ⏰8am-1am; 📶; 🚊1/2/5/14 Dam/Paleisstraat) are long-standing favourites.

D'Vijff Vlieghen (p33)

Drinking

In 't Aepjen

BROWN CAFE

17 Map p28, E3

Candles burn even during the day in this 15th-century building – one of two remaining wooden buildings in the city – which has been a tavern since 1519: in the 16th and 17th centuries it served as an inn for sailors from the Far East, who often brought *aapjes* (monkeys) to trade for lodging. Vintage jazz on the stereo enhances the time-warp feel. (Zeedijk 1; ⏰noon-1am Mon-Thu, to 3am Fri & Sat; 🚊1/2/4/5/9/13/16/17/24 Centraal Station)

Tales & Spirits

COCKTAIL BAR

18 🍷 Map p28, B3

Chandeliers glitter beneath wooden beams at Tales & Spirits, which creates its own house infusions, syrups and vinegar-based shrubs. Craft cocktails such as Floats Like a Butterfly (orange vodka, peach liqueur, saffron honey and lemon sorbet) and Stings Like a Bee (Dijon gin, cognac, maple syrup and soda water) are served in vintage and one-of-a-kind glasses. Minimum age is 21. (www.talesandspirits. com; Lijnbaanssteeg 5-7; ⏰5.30pm-1am Tue-Thu & Sun, to 3am Fri & Sat; 🚊1/2/5/13/17 Nieuwezijds Kolk)

Cut Throat
BAR

19 Map p28, C4

Beneath 1930s arched brick ceilings, Cut Throat ingeniously combines a men's barbering service (book ahead) with a happening bar serving international craft beers, cocktails including infused G&Ts (such as blueberry and thyme or mandarin and rosemary), 'spiked' milkshakes and coffee from Amsterdam roastery De Wasserette. Brunch stretches to 4pm daily; all-day dishes span fried chicken and waffles, and surf-and-turf burgers. (☎06 2534 3769; www.cutthroatbarber.nl; Beursplein 5; ☺bar 9.30am-1am Sun-Thu, to 3am Fri & Sat, barber 11am-8pm Mon-Thu, 11am-7pm Fri, 10am-6pm Sat, noon-6pm Sun; ☞; ☒4/9/24 Rokin)

Dum Dum Palace
COCKTAIL BAR

20 Map p28, E3

Asian takes on classic cocktails at this designer spot include a Tom Yam Collins, green-tea mojito, Tokyo Sling, five-spice whisky sour and black-sesame martini. Drinks are served in its main skylit room and in a secret bar out back (ask the staff to show you through). Food-truck caterers HotMamaHot collaborate in the kitchen, serving four kinds of dumplings. (www.dumdum.nl; Zeedijk 37; ☺11am-1am Sun-Thu, to 3am Fri & Sat; ☞; ☒1/2/4/5/9/13/16/17/24 Centraal Station)

Brouwerij De Prael
BREWERY

21 Map p28, D3

Sample organic beers (Scotch ale, IPA, barley wine and many more varieties) at the socially minded De Prael brewery (p30), known for employing people with a history of mental illness. Its multilevel tasting room has comfy couches and big wooden tables strewn about. There's often live music. A four-beer tasting flight costs €10. (www.deprael.nl; Oudezijds Armsteeg 26; ☺noon-midnight Mon-Wed, to 1am Thu-Sat, to 11pm Sun; ☒1/2/4/5/9/13/16/17/24 Centraal Station)

In de Olofspoort
BROWN CAFE

22 Map p28, D3

The door of this brown cafe–tasting room dating from 1618 was once the city gate. It stocks over 200 *jenevers* (Dutch gins), liqueurs and bitters; check out the extraordinary selection behind the back-room bar. You can also buy its unique tipples at its onsite shop, which opens until 10pm. Occasional singalongs add to the spirited atmosphere. (www.olofspoort. com; Nieuwebrugsteeg 13; ☺4pm-12.30am Tue-Thu, 3pm-1.30am Fri & Sat, 3-10pm Sun; ☒4/9/16/24 Centraal Station)

Wynand Fockink
DISTILLERY

23 Map p28, C5

Dating from 1679, this small tasting house in an arcade behind Grand Hotel Krasnapolsky serves scores of *jenevers* (Dutch gins) and liqueurs.

Although there's no seating, it's an intimate place to knock back a shot glass or two. At weekends, guides give 45-minute distillery tours (in English) that are followed by six tastings; reserve online. (📞020-639 26 95; http://wynand-fockink.nl; Pijlsteeg 31; tours €17.50; ⏰tasting tavern 3-9pm daily, tours 3pm, 4.30pm, 6pm & 7.30pm Sat & Sun; 🚋4/9/16/24 Dam)

Hoppe
BROWN CAFE

24 🚇 Map p28, A8

An Amsterdam institution, Hoppe has been filling glasses since 1670. Barflies and raconteurs toss back brews amid the ancient wood panelling of the brown cafe at No 18 and the more modern, early-20th-century pub at No 20. In all but the iciest weather, the energetic crowd spills out from the dark interior and onto the Spui. (http://cafehoppe.com; Spui 18-20; ⏰8am-1am Sun-Thu, to 2am Fri & Sat; 🚋1/2/5 Spui)

De Blauwe Parade
BAR

25 🚇 Map p28, A4

A frieze of Delft blue-and-white tiles – the world's largest Delft-tile tableau – wraps around the walls above beautiful wood panelling at this exquisite bar (a listed monument) within the **Die Port van Cleve** (📞020-714 20 00; www.dieportvancleve.com; d from €179; ✳@🛜) hotel. Regular events include tasting sessions of liqueurs on Monday and *jenevers* (gins) on Wednesday

Art & Book Markets

Save on gallery fees by buying direct from the artists at Amsterdam's weekly **art market** (Map p28, A7; http://artplein-spui.com; Spui; ⏰11am-6.30pm Sun Mar-Dec; 🚋1/2/5 Spui). Some 60 Dutch and contemporary artists set up on the square. Old tomes, maps and sheet music are the speciality at the daily (bar Sunday) **Oudemanhuispoort Book Market** (Map p28, C7; Oudemanhuispoort; ⏰11am-4pm Mon-Sat; 🚋4/9/14/16/24 Spui/Rokin).

(both from 7pm), where you pay by the glass. (http://deblauweparade.com; Nieuwezijds Voorburgwal 178; ⏰noon-midnight; 🛜; 🚋1/2/5/13/14/17 Dam)

't Mandje
GAY

26 🚇 Map p28, E4

Amsterdam's oldest gay bar opened in 1927, then shut in 1982 when the Zeedijk grew too seedy. But its trinket-covered interior was lovingly dusted every week until it reopened in 2008. The devoted bartenders can tell you stories about the bar's brassy lesbian founder Bet van Beeren. It's one of the most *gezellig* (cosy, convivial) places in the centre, gay or straight. (www.cafetmandje.amsterdam; Zeedijk 63; ⏰4pm-1am Tue-Thu, 3pm-3am Fri & Sat, to 1am Sun; 🚋1/2/4/5/9/13/16/17/24 Centraal Station)

Understand

The Smoking Lowdown

Cannabis is not technically legal in the Netherlands – yet it is widely tolerated. Here's the deal: the possession and purchase of small amounts (5g) of 'soft drugs' (ie marijuana, hashish, space cakes and mushroom-based truffles) is allowed, and users aren't prosecuted for smoking or carrying this amount. This means that coffeeshops are actually conducting an illegal business – but again, it is tolerated to a certain extent.

Products For Sale

Most cannabis products sold in the Netherlands used to be imported, but today the country has high-grade home produce, so-called *nederwiet*. It's a particularly strong product – the most potent varieties contain 15% tetrahydrocannabinol (THC), the active substance that gets people high (since 2011, anything above 15% is classified as a hard drug and therefore illegal). In a nutshell, Dutch weed will literally blow your mind – perhaps to an extent that isn't altogether pleasant. Newbies to smoking pot and hash should exercise caution. Space cakes and cookies (baked goods made with hash or marijuana) are also sold in coffeeshops. Most shops offer rolling papers, pipes or bongs to use; you can also buy ready-made joints.

Dos & Don'ts

Do ask coffeeshop staff for advice on what and how to consume, and heed it, even if nothing happens after an hour. And do ask staff for the menu of products on offer. Don't drink alcohol (it's illegal in coffeeshops) and don't smoke tobacco, whether mixed with marijuana or on its own. It is forbidden in accordance with the Netherlands' laws.

Coffeeshop Closures

Amsterdam currently has 173 coffeeshops (30% of the Netherlands' total), which is down from a high of 350 in 1995. In some areas of the country, foreigners are banned from coffeeshops. Not so in Amsterdam. Coffeeshops are a big part of Amsterdam's tourism business, with around one-third of travellers visiting the smoky venues. Nonetheless, a number have closed as rules went into effect that shut down coffeeshops operating near schools.

GRANT ROONEY/AGE FOTOSTOCK ©

Casa Rosso

Entertainment

Bitterzoet

LIVE MUSIC

27 ⭐ Map p28, C2

Always full, always changing, this venue with a capacity of just 350 people is one of the friendliest places in town, and has a diverse crowd. Music (sometimes live, sometimes courtesy of a DJ) can be funk, roots, drum 'n' bass, Latin, Afro-beat, old-school jazz or hip-hop groove. (📞020-421 23 18; www.bitterzoet.com; Spuistraat 2; ⏰8pm-late; 🚃1/2/5/13/17 Nieuwezijds Kolk)

De Brakke Grond

THEATRE

28 ⭐ Map p28, C6

De Brakke Grond sponsors a fantastic array of music, experimental video, modern dance and exciting young theatre at its nifty performance hall in the Flemish Cultural Centre. Upcoming events are listed on its website. (📞020-622 90 14; www.brakkegrond. nl; Flemish Cultural Centre, Nes 43; 🛜; 🚃4/9/14/16/24 Rokin)

Casa Rosso

LIVE PERFORMANCE

29 ⭐ Map p28, D5

It might be stretching it to describe a live sex show as 'classy', but this theatre is clean and comfortable and always packed with couples and hen's-night parties. Acts can be male, female, both or lesbian (although not gay...sorry, boys!). Performers demonstrate everything from positions of the Kama Sutra to pole dances and incredible tricks with lit candles. (www.casarosso.nl; Oudezijds Achterburgwal 106-108; admission with/without drinks €55/45; ⏲7pm-2am Sun-Thu, to 3am Fri & Sat; 🚊4/9/16/24 Dam)

Shopping

X Bank   DESIGN

30 🔒 Map p28, A5

More than just a concept store showcasing Dutch-designed haute couture and ready-to-wear fashion, furniture, art, gadgets and homewares, the 700-sq-metre X Bank – in a former bank that's now part of the striking **W Amsterdam** (☎020-811 25 00; www.wamsterdam.com; Spuistraat 175; d/ste from €370/567; ❄@🛜🏊) hotel – also hosts exhibitions, workshops, launches and lectures. Interior displays change every month; check the website for upcoming events. (http://xbank.amsterdam; Spuistraat 172; ⏲10am-6pm Mon-Wed, to 9pm Thu-Sat, noon-8pm Sun; 🚊1/2/5/13/17 Dam)

Mark Raven Grafiek   GIFTS & SOUVENIRS

31 🔒 Map p28, B4

Artist Mark Raven's distinctive vision of Amsterdam is available on posters, coasters and stylish T-shirts that make great souvenirs. Prices are impressively reasonable and there's often a sale rack out front. (www.markraven.nl; Nieuwezijds Voorburgwal 174; ⏲10.30am-6pm; 🚊1/2/5/13/14/17 Dam/Raadhuisstraat)

By AMFI   FASHION & ACCESSORIES

32 🔒 Map p28, A8

Students, teachers and alumni of the Amsterdam Fashion Institute show and sell their wares at this small boutique. It's mostly clothing and decor wildly inventive in style but sure to be one of a kind. (http://amfi.nl/byamfi; Spui 23; ⏲1-6pm Mon-Fri, hours vary Sat; 🚊1/2/5 Spui)

Condomerie Het Gulden Vlies   ADULT

33 🔒 Map p28, C5

In the heart of the Red Light District, this brightly lit boutique sells condoms in every imaginable size, colour, flavour and design (horned devils, marijuana leaves, Delftware tiles...), along with lubricants and saucy gifts. Photos aren't allowed inside the shop. (https://condomerie.com; Warmoesstraat 141; ⏲11am-9pm Mon & Wed-Sat, to 6pm Tue, 1-6pm Sun; 🚊4/9/14/16/24 Dam)

De Bijenkorf   DEPARTMENT STORE

34 🔒 Map p28, B5

Amsterdam's most fashionable department store has a grander exterior than interior, but it occupies the city's highest-profile location, facing

De Bijenkorf

the Royal Palace (p24). Shoppers will enjoy the well-chosen clothing, cosmetics, accessories, toys, homewares and books. The snazzy cafe on the 5th floor has a terrace with steeple views. (www.debijenkorf.nl; Dam 1; ⏱11am-8pm Sun & Mon, 10am-8pm Tue & Wed, 10am-9pm Thu & Fri, 9.30am-8pm Sat; 🚊4/9/16/24 Dam)

Kokopelli
ADULT

35 🔒 Map p28, D3

Were it not for its trade in 'magic truffles' (similar to the now-outlawed psilocybin mushrooms, aka 'magic mushrooms'), you might swear this large, beautiful space was a fashionable clothing or homewares store. There's a coffee and juice bar and a chill-out lounge area overlooking Damrak. (www.kokopelli.nl; Warmoesstraat 12; ⏱11am-10pm; 🚊4/9/16/24 Centraal Station)

Mr B
ADULT

36 🔒 Map p28, D4

Kinky! The tamer wares at this renowned Red Light District shop dating from 1994 include leather and rubber suits, hoods and bondage equipment, all made to measure if you want. Mind-boggling sex toys add a playful (and somewhat scary) element. (www.misterb.com; Warmoesstraat 89; ⏱11am-7pm Mon-Wed, to 8pm Thu-Sat, 1-6pm Sun; 🚊4/9/16/24 Dam)

Explore

Jordaan & the Western Canal Ring

If Amsterdam's neighbourhoods held a 'best personality' contest, the Jordaan would surely win. Its intimacy is contagious, with jovial bar singalongs, candlelit *bruin cafés* and flower-box-adorned eateries spilling out onto narrow streets. The Western Canal Ring's waterways flow next door. Grand old buildings and oddball speciality shops line the glinting waterways. Roaming around them can cause days to vanish.

The Sights in a Day

☀️ Do the Dutch thing and carve into a hulking pancake at, well, **Pancakes!** (p55). Poke around the surrounding shops, then cross over Prinsengracht to see what life on the water is like at the **Houseboat Museum** (p51).

☀️ Devote the afternoon to the neighbourhood's gorgeous canals. Visit **Het Grachtenhuis** (p50), which tells the story of the 400-year-old waterways and their engineering genius. Afterwards walk along the Herengracht and ogle the Golden Age manors rising up along the canal. Enjoy an opulent canalside lunch at **De Belhamel** (p53). Photography buffs can see what's on at **Huis Marseille** (p50).

🌙 Head over to the **Anne Frank Huis** (p44) in the early evening, when crowds are thinnest. For dinner, head to mod-rustic **Balthazar's Keuken** (p53) for the daily special, or gastronomy at **Wolf Atelier** (p52). Then take your pick of brown cafés for a nightcap. **'t Smalle** (p55) always hosts a high-spirited group. Or croon with the crowd at **De Twee Zwaantjes** (p56).

For a local's day in Jordaan, see p46.

 Top Sights

Anne Frank Huis (p44)

🔍 **Local Life**

Shopping the Jordaan & Western Canal Ring (p46)

💜 **Best of Amsterdam**

Best Shopping
Noordermarkt (p47)

Frozen Fountain (p60)

Galleria d'Arte Rinascimento (p62)

Best For Kids
Het Oud-Hollandsch Snoepwinkeltje (p61)

Mechanisch Speelgoed (p62)

Getting There

🚊 **Tram** Trams 13, 14 and 17 have stops near the Western Canal Ring's main attractions; any tram or bus that stops near the Dam is just a short walk away. Trams 3 and 10 along Marnixstraat skirt the Jordaan's western edge; trams 13, 14 and 17 along Rozengracht traverse its centre.

⚓ **Boat** The Canal Bus stop near Westermarkt is handy for the Anne Frank Huis.

Top Sights
Anne Frank Huis

It is one of the 20th century's most compelling stories: a young Jewish girl forced into hiding with her family and their friends to escape deportation by the Nazis. The house they used as a hideaway should be a highlight of any visit to Amsterdam; indeed, it attracts more than one million visitors a year.

👁 Map p48, C4

📞 020-556 71 05

www.annefrank.org

Prinsengracht 263-267

adult/child €9/4.50

🕐 9am-10pm Apr-Oct, 9am-7pm Sun-Fri, to 9pm Sat Nov-Mar

🚊 13/14/17 Westermarkt

The Occupants

The Franks – father Otto, mother Edith, older sister Margot and Anne – moved into the hidden chambers in July 1942, along with Mr and Mrs van Pels (whom Anne called the van Daans in her diary) and their son Peter. Four months later Fritz Pfeffer (aka Albert van Dussel) joined the household. The group lived there until they were betrayed to the Gestapo in August 1944.

Offices & Warehouse

The building originally held Otto Frank's pectin (a substance used in jelly-making) business. On the lower floors you'll see the former offices of Victor Kugler, Otto's business partner; and the desks of Miep Gies, Bep Voskuijl and Jo Kleiman, all of whom worked in the office and provided food, clothing and other goods for the household.

Secret Annexe

The upper floors in the *Achterhuis* (rear house) contain the Secret Annexe, where the living quarters have been preserved in powerful austerity. As you enter Anne's small bedroom, you can still see the remnants of a young girl's dreams; the photos of Hollywood stars and postcards of the Dutch royal family she pasted on the wall.

The Diary

More haunting exhibits and videos await after you return to the front house – including Anne's red-plaid diary itself, sitting alone in its glass case. Watch the video of Anne's old schoolmate Hanneli Goslar, who describes encountering Anne at Bergen-Belsen. Read heartbreaking letters from Otto, the only Secret Annexe occupant to survive the concentration camps.

☑ Top Tips

▶ At the time of research, the only way to visit was with a ticket purchased online, although this may change; check the website. Tickets are released in phases, from two months in advance until the day itself (subject to availability; be warned that the demand is often greater than the supply). You can print them or show them on your phone. You'll receive a set time for entry.

▶ In spring and summer, take advantage of the later evening hours of the Anne Frank Huis.

✕ Take a Break

Bistro Bij Ons (p53) serves classic Dutch dishes in charming surrounds.

For a quick, filling snack, head to famous *frites* (fries) stand Wil Graanstra Friteshuis (p53).

Local Life
Shopping the Jordaan & Western Canal Ring

These are Amsterdam's prime neighbourhoods to stumble upon offbeat little shops selling items you'd find nowhere else. Velvet ribbons? Herb-spiced Gouda? Vintage jewellery? They're all here amid the Western Canals' quirky stores and the Jordaan's eclectic boutiques and markets. Everything is squashed into a grid of tiny lanes – a perfect place to lose yourself for an afternoon stroll.

....

1 Antiqueing at Antiekcentrum

Anyone who likes peculiar old stuff might enter **Antiekcentrum Amsterdam** (Amsterdam Antique Centre; www.antiekcentrumamsterdam. nl; Elandsgracht 109; ⏰11am-6pm Mon-Fri, to 5pm Sat & Sun; ▣7/10/17 Elandsgracht), a knick-knack mini-mall, and never come out. You're just as likely to find 1940s

silk dresses as you are 1970s Swedish porn. Brasserie Blazer serves well-priced French fare inside to fuel the browsing.

❷ Tunes at Johnny Jordaanplein

The small square **Johnny Jordaanplein** (cnr Prinsengracht & Elandsgracht; 🚊13/14/17 Westermarkt) is dedicated to the local hero and musician who sang the romantic music known as *levenslied* (tears-in-your-beer-style ballads). There are bronze busts of Johnny and his band, but the real star here is the colourful utility hut splashed with nostalgic lyrics.

❸ Wander the Negen Straatjes

The **Negen Straatjes** (Nine Streets; www.de9straatjes.nl; 🚊1/2/5 Spui) comprise a tic-tac-toe board of wee shops dealing in vintage fashions, housewares and oddball specialities such as antique eyeglass frames. It's bounded by Reestraat, Hartenstraat and Gasthuismolensteeg to the north and Runstraat, Huidenstraat and Wijde Heisteeg to the south. Bonus points if you find the doll doctor!

❹ Refuel at Brix

The loungey setting makes **Brix Food 'n' Drinx** (www.cafebrix.nl; Wolvenstraat 16; ⏰9am-1am Sun-Thu, to 3am Fri & Sat; 🚊1/2/5 Spui) a great place to chill over cocktails (including three different Bloody Marys) or sample the astutely chosen wines. There's live soul, blues and jazz on Mondays from about 7pm.

❺ Rummage the Noordermarkt

The **Noordermarkt** (Northern Market; www.jordaanmarkten.nl; ⏰flea market 9am-1pm Mon, farmers market 9am-4pm Sat; 🚊3/10 Marnixplein) surrounds the Noorderkerk and hosts two bazaars. On Monday mornings it's a trove of secondhand clothing (great rummage piles) and assorted antique trinkets. On Saturdays, most of the clothing stalls are replaced by gorgeous produce and *kaas* (cheese) from growers around Amsterdam.

❻ Get Hip on Haarlemmerdijk

The street **Haarlemmerdijk** buzzes with stylish shops and lots of places to snack or unwind over a drink. It is a culinary destination, not just for restaurants but for its slew of gourmet provisions and kitchen shops. Keep an eye out for hip lolly makers, cookbook vendors and tea emporiums among the retailers.

❼ Relax at De Kat in de Wijngaert

De Kat in de Wijngaert (www.dekatindewijngaert.nl; Lindengracht 160; ⏰10am-1am Sun-Thu, to 3am Fri, 9am-3am Sat; 🚊3/10 Marnixplein) is the kind of *bruin café* where one beer soon turns into half a dozen – maybe it's the influence of the old-guard arts types who hang out here. Try soaking it up with what many people vote as the best *tosti* (toasted sandwich) in town.

Westerdoksdijk

E

Westerdokskade

Westerdok

10 ❌

18,22

Haarlemmerplein

P

Binnen Dommersstr
Mouthaanst

21 ⊙

39 ⊙

Haarlemmerdijk Vinkenstr

Binnen Oranjestr

Korte Prinsengr

Haarlemmer Houttuinen

Brouwersgr

Binnen Brouwersstr

Haarlemmerstr

Heren- markt

Binnen Wieringerstr

Herengr Langestr

Kor-je spoortst

Korte Kolkst

Singel

Singel

Spuistr

Voorburgwal

14 ❌

11 ❌

Herengr

Keizersgr

Herenstr

Prinsenstr

Keizersgr

Herenstr

Blauwburgwal

Bergstr

20 ⊙

Herengracht

Keizersgracht

Leliegr

Leliegr

40 ⊙

Amsterdam Tulip Museum

8 ⊙

Anne Frank Huis ◆

Prinsengracht

24 ⊙

9 ⊙ Noorderkerk

Noordermarkt

16 ❌

1e Lindenswarsstr

Boomstr

4 ⊙

Pianola Museum 37 ⊙

1e Egelantiers dwarsstr

26 ⊙

19 ⊙

17 ⊙

Electric ⊙ 6 Ladyland

Egelantiersgracht

D

C

B

A

400 m

0.2 miles

Haarlemmerplein

Brouwersgr

30 ⊙

Palmgr

Palmdwarsstr

Palmstr

Goudsbloemstr

Willemsstr

1e Lindendwarsstr

2e Lindendwarsstr

Lindengr · Noorderstr

Kartuizersstr

Tichelstr

Lijnbaansgr

1e Anjeliersdwarsstr

33 ⊙

15 ❌

JORDAAN

36 ⊙ 35 ⊙

2e Egelantiersdwarsstr

1e Egelantiersstr

2e Egelantiersdwarsstr

2e Tuind warsstr

Tuinstr

Anjeliersstr

Marnixstr

1e Marnix plantsoen

Marnixstr

Lijnbaansgr

Lijnbaansstr

Lijnbaansgr

1e Nassaustr

Nassaukade

Westerstr

2e Anjeliersdwarsstr

Marnixstr

Nassaukade

Marnixkade

Kattenslool Jacob Catskade

Fagelstr

Streichstraat Marnixkade

Lod Tripstr

Frederik Hendrik plagsoen

Nassaukade

Van Oldenbarneveldtstr

Jan Oldenbarneveldtstr

Frederik Hendrikstr

Marnixstr

Nassaukade

Frederik Hendrikstr

1

2

3

4

Nieuwendijk

Dam

Damrak

Oude Turfmarkt

Rokin

Vijzelstr

Kalverstr

Spui

Nieuwezijds Voorburgwal

Voetboogstr
Heiligeweg
Handboogstr

Singel
Singel
Singel

Reguliersdwarsstr

Herengr
Herengr

Nieuwendijk

Spuistraat
Nieuwezijds

Torensluis

Oude Leliestr

Raadhuisstr

Paleisstr
Wijdest

Gasthuis-
molenst

Hartenstr
Reestr

Herengr
Herengr

Singel
Singel

Wijde Heist
Wijdest

Wolvenstr

Keizersgr
Keizersgr

Beulingstr

34

Huidenstr
Bijbels
Museum 7

2 Huis Marseille
3

Herengracht

Koningsplein

Keizersgracht

Keizersgr
125

Leidsestr

Kerkstr

Runstr
42

Het Grachtenhuis 32

Prinsengr
Prinsengr

Westerkerk 1
Westermarkt

13

Prinsengr

Reestr
Berenstr

Molenpad

Prinsengracht

41
18

5 Houseboat
Museum

Looiersgracht

Raamplein
23

38

1e Bloem-
dwarsstr

Rozengr

1e Rozendwarsstr

Konijnen
str

Oude Looiersstr

Elandsgr

Passeerdersstr

Passeerdersgr
Passeerdersstr

Bloemgr

Rozenstr

Laurierstr
Lauriergr

Hazenstr

Elandsstr
12

Oude Looiersstr
Elandsgr

Lijnbaansgr

7,10

2e Bloem-
dwarssstr

13,14,17

25 28

2e Laurierdwarsstr

Laurierstr

37

Lijnbaansgracht

Lijnbaansgr

Marnixstr

22

Singelgracht

Nassaukade

OUD
WEST

Hugo de
Grootstr

29

De Clercqstr

Da Costastr

Da Costagracht
Da Costagracht

Kinkerstr

27

Bilderdijkstr

Bosboom
Toussaintstr

Jacob van Lennepkade
Jacob van Lennepstr

Sights

Westerkerk
CHURCH

1 ⊙ Map p48, C5

The main gathering place for Amsterdam's Dutch Reformed community, this church was built for rich Protestants to a 1620 design by Hendrick de Keyser. The nave is the largest in the Netherlands and is covered by a wooden barrel vault. The huge main organ dates from 1686, with panels decorated with instruments and biblical scenes. Rembrandt (1606–69), who died bankrupt at nearby Rozengracht, was buried in a pauper's grave somewhere in the church. Its **bell tower** (tours €7; ⊙10am-7.30pm Mon-Sat Jun-Sep) can be climbed. (Western Church; ☏020-624 77 66; www.westerkerk.nl; Prinsengracht 281; ⊙11am-4pm Mon-Sat May-Sep, Mon-Fri Oct-Apr; 🚊13/14/17 Westermarkt)

Het Grachtenhuis
MUSEUM

2 ⊙ Map p48, D7

Learn about the remarkable feat of engineering behind the Canal Ring through this museum's holograms, videos, models, cartoons, scale model of Amsterdam and other innovative exhibits, which explain how the canals and the houses that line them were built. Unlike at most Amsterdam museums, you can't simply wander through: small groups go in together to experience the multimedia exhibits. It takes about 45 minutes, and you'll come out knowing why Amsterdam's houses tilt. Online tickets are up to €2 cheaper. (Canal House; ☏020-421 16 56; www.hetgrachtenhuis.nl; Herengracht 386; adult/child €12/6; ⊙10am-5pm Tue-Sun; 🚊1/2/5 Koningsplein)

Huis Marseille
MUSEUM

3 ⊙ Map p48, D7

Large-scale temporary exhibitions from its own collection are staged at this well-curated photography museum, which also hosts travelling shows. Themes might include portraiture, nature or regional photography, and exhibitions are spread out over several floors and in a summer house behind the main house. French merchant Isaac Focquier built Huis Marseille in 1665, installing a map of the French port Marseille on the facade. The original structure has remained largely intact. (☏020-531 89 89; www.huismarseille.nl; Keizersgracht 401; adult/child €8/free; ⊙11am-6pm Tue-Sun; 🚊1/2/5 Keizersgracht)

Pianola Museum
MUSEUM

4 ⊙ Map p48, C3

This is a very special place, crammed with pianolas from the early 1900s. The museum has around 50, although only a dozen are on display at any given time, as well as some 30,000 music rolls and a player pipe organ. The curator gives an hour-long guided tour and music demonstrations with great zest. Regular concerts are held on the player pianos, featuring anything from Mozart to Fats Waller and rare classical or jazz tunes composed especially for the instrument. (☏020-627 96 24; www.pianola.nl; Westerstraat 106; museum

TUPUNGATO/SHUTTERSTOCK ©

Amsterdam Tulip Museum (p52)

adult/child €5/3, concert tickets from €7.50;
🕐2-5pm Sun; 🚊3/10 Marnixplein)

Houseboat Museum   MUSEUM

5 ⊙ Map p48, C6

This quirky museum, a 23m-long
sailing barge from 1914, offers a good
sense of how *gezellig* (cosy) life can be
on the water. The actual displays are
minimal, but you can watch a presentation on houseboats (some pretty and
some ghastly) and inspect the sleeping,
living, cooking and dining quarters
with all the mod cons. Cash only.
(📞020-427 07 50; www.houseboatmuseum.nl;
Prinsengracht 296k; adult/child €4.50/3.50;
🕐10am-5pm Jul & Aug, 10am-5pm Tue-Sun
Sep-Dec & Feb-Jun; 🚊13/14/17 Westermarkt)

Electric Ladyland   MUSEUM

6 ⊙ Map p48, C4

The world's first museum of
fluorescent art features owner Nick
Padalino's psychedelic sculpture work
on one side and cases of naturally
luminescent rocks and manufactured
glowing objects (money, government
ID cards, etc) on the other. Jimi
Hendrix, the Beatles and other trippy
artists play on the stereo while Nick
lovingly describes each item in the
collection. His art gallery–shop is
upstairs. (www.electric-lady-land.com;
2e Leliedwarsstraat 5; adult/child €5/free;
🕐2-6pm Wed-Sat; 🚊13/14/17 Westermarkt)

Bijbels Museum

MUSEUM

7 Map p48, D7

A scale model of the Jewish Tabernacle described in Exodus – built by dedicated minister Leendert Schouten and drawing thousands of visitors even before it was completed in 1851 – is the star attraction at this bible museum. Inside a 1622 canal house, the museum has an extraordinary collection of bibles, including the Netherlands' oldest, a 1477-printed Delft Bible, and a 1st edition of the 1637 Dutch authorised version. Trees and plants mentioned in the Good Book feature in the garden. (Bible Museum; www.bijbelsmuseum.nl; Herengracht 366-368; adult/child €8.50/4.25; ⊙11am-5pm Tue-Sun; 🚊1/2/5 Spui)

Amsterdam Tulip Museum

MUSEUM

8 Map p48, C4

Allow around half an hour at the diminutive Amsterdam Tulip Museum, which offers a nifty overview of the history of the country's favourite bloom. Through exhibits, timelines and two short films (in English), you'll learn how Ottoman merchants encountered the flowers in the Himalayan steppes and began commercial production in Turkey, how fortunes were made and lost during Dutch 'Tulipmania' in the 17th century, and how bulbs were used as food during the war. You'll also discover present-day growing and harvesting techniques. (📞020-421 00 95; www.amsterdamtulipmuseum.com; Prinsengracht 116; adult/child €5/3; ⊙10am-6pm; 🚊13/14/17 Westermarkt)

Noorderkerk

CHURCH

9 Map p48, D3

Near the Prinsengracht's northern end, this imposing Calvinist church was completed in 1623 for the 'common' people in the Jordaan. (The upper classes attended the Westerkerk further south.) It was built in the shape of a broad Greek cross (four arms of equal length) around a central pulpit, giving the entire congregation unimpeded access. Hendrick de Keyser's design, unusual at the time, would become common for Protestant churches throughout the country. It hosts the well-regarded Saturday-afternoon **Noorderkerkconcerten** (📞020-620 44 15; https://noorderkerkconcerten.nl/concerten; tickets from €16; ⊙2pm Sat) concert series. (Northern Church; www.noorderkerk.org; Noordermarkt 48; ⊙10.30am-12.30pm Mon, 11am-1pm Sat; 🚊3/10 Marnixplein)

Eating

Wolf Atelier

GASTRONOMY €€

10 Map p48, E1

Atop a 1920 railway swing bridge, a glass box with pivoting windows is the showcase for experimental Austrian chef Michael Wolf's 'tartar-ia' (serving six styles of tartar, including steak, tuna and salmon, each in three sizes) and 'atelier' (workshop), where he creates wild flavour combinations. The 360-degree views are magical at night; you can linger for a drink until 1am. (📞020-344 64 28; www.wolfatelier.nl; Westerdoksplein 20; mains €24, 4-/5-/15-course menus €42.50/48/75; ⊙noon-5pm & 6-10pm Mon-Sat; 🚊48 Westerdoksdijk)

De Belhamel
EUROPEAN €€

11 Map p48, E3

In warm weather the canalside tables here at the head of the Herengracht are an aphrodisiac, and the richly wallpapered art-nouveau interior set over two levels provides the perfect backdrop for exquisitely presented dishes such as poached sole with wild-spinach bisque, veal sweetbreads with crispy bacon, onion confit and deep-fried sage, or a half lobster with velvety salmon mayonnaise. (✆020-622 10 95; www.belhamel.nl; Brouwersgracht 60; mains €23.50-26.50, 3-/4-course menus €35/45; ⊙noon-4pm & 6-10pm Sun-Thu, to 10.30pm Fri & Sat; 🚊18/21/22 Buiten Brouwersstraat)

Balthazar's Keuken
MEDITERRANEAN €€

12 Map p48, B7

In a former blacksmith's forge, with a modern-rustic look and an open kitchen, this is consistently one of Amsterdam's top-rated restaurants. Don't expect a wide-ranging menu: the philosophy is basically 'whatever we have on hand', which might mean wild sea bass with mushroom risotto, or confit of rabbit, but it's invariably delectable. Reservations recommended. (✆020-420 21 14; www.balthazarskeuken.nl; Elandsgracht 108; 3-course menu €34.50; ⊙6-10.30pm Tue-Sun; 🚊7/10/17 Elandsgracht)

Bistro Bij Ons
DUTCH €€

13 Map p48, C5

If you're not in town visiting your Dutch *oma* (grandma), try the honest-to-goodness cooking at this charming retro bistro instead. Classics include *stamppot* (potatoes mashed with another vegetable) with sausage, *raasdonders* (split peas with bacon, onion and pickles) and *poffertjes* (small pancakes with butter and powdered sugar). House-made liqueurs include plum and *drop* (liquorice) varieties. (✆020-627 90 16; http://bistrobijons.nl; Prinsengracht 287; mains €14-19.50; ⊙10am-10pm Tue-Sun; 🐾; 🚊13/14/17 Westermarkt)

Vinnies Deli
CAFE €

14 Map p48, E2

Only organic, locally sourced produce is used in Vinnies' extensive breakfasts, gourmet sandwiches, lush salads, hot specials such as kale-and-mushroom

Local Life
Frites
Amsterdammers swear by the crispy spuds at **Wil Graanstra Friteshuis** (Map p48, C5; Westermarkt 11; frites €2.50-4, sauce €0.50; ⊙noon-7pm Mon-Sat; 🚊13/14/17 Westermarkt). The family-run business has been frying on the square by the Westerkerk since 1956. Most locals top their cones with mayonnaise, though *oorlog* (a peanut sauce–mayo combo), curry sauce and piccalilli (relish) rock the taste buds, too.

Top Tip

Cheese Tasting

Here's your chance to become a *kaas* (cheese) connoisseur. Century-old Dutch cheesemaker **Reypenaer** (Map p48, D5; ☎020-320 63 33; www.reypenaercheese.com; Singel 182; tastings from €16.50; ⏰tastings by reservation; ☒1/2/5/13/14/17 Dam) offers tastings in a rustic classroom beneath its shop. The hour-long session includes six cheeses – two goat's milk, four cow's milk – from young to old, with wine and port pairings. Expert staff members guide you through them, helping you appreciate the cheeses' look, aroma and taste.

frittata or roasted miso-marinated aubergine, and creative cakes; the coffee is from Amsterdam roastery Bocca. Vegan options abound. If you're imagining the designer furniture in your lounge room, you're in luck: all the pieces are for sale. (http://vinnieshomepage.com; Haarlemmerstraat 46; mains €7.50-12.50; ⏰8am-5pm; ☒; ☒1/2/4/5/9/13/16/17/24 Centraal Station)

Trattoria di Donna Sofia   ITALIAN €€

15 Map p48, C3

With rustic decor and white-clothed tables, Donna Sofia – named for the owner's grandmother – has a daily-changing blackboard menu of Neapolitan dishes chalked in Italian. Pastas are made in-house and risottos are

a speciality; fresh herbs enhance the flavours of the fish, meat and vegetarian dishes. All-Italian vintages feature on the small but well-chosen wine list. (☎020-623 41 04; www.trattoriadidonnasofia.com; Anjeliersstraat 300; mains €14-28; ⏰5-11pm Mon-Sat; ☒3/10 Marnixplein)

Winkel   CAFE €

16 Map p48, D3

This sprawling, indoor-outdoor space is great for people-watching, popular for coffees and small meals (such as wild-boar stew with sauerkraut and cranberry sauce), and out-of-the-park for its tall, cakey apple pie, served with clouds of whipped cream. On market days (Monday and Saturday) there's almost always a queue out the door. (www.winkel43.nl; Noordermarkt 43; dishes €3.40-7, mains €8-16.50; ⏰kitchen 7am-10pm Mon & Sat, 8am-10pm Tue-Fri, 10am-10pm Sun, bar to 1am Sun-Thu, to 3am Fri & Sat; ☒3/10 Marnixplein)

De Reiger   DUTCH €€

17 Map p48, C4

Assiduously local and very atmospheric, this corner *café* (pub) – one of the Jordaan's oldest, with high beamed ceilings and art-nouveau and art-deco fittings – has a quiet front bar and a noisy, more spacious dining section at the back serving a short but stunning menu (venison and stewed pear with honey-cinnamon sauce, for instance). No reservations or credit cards. (http://dereigeramsterdam.nl; Nieuwe Leliestraat 34; mains €18.50-24; ⏰5-9.30pm Mon-Fri,

SARAH COGHILL/LONELY PLANET ©

Wine and cheese tasting at Reypenaer

noon-9.30pm Sat, 4-8pm Sun, bar to 11.30pm Mon-Fri, to 10.30pm Sat & Sun; ☐13/14/17 Westermarkt)

Pancakes!

DUTCH €

18 Map p48, C6

The blue-tile tables at snug little Pancakes! are always packed with diners tucking into the signature dish, whether sweet (apple, nuts and cinnamon) or savoury (ham, chicory and Camembert cheese). Gluten-free pancakes are also available. Smiley-face pancakes are a favourite with kids. (☎020-528 97 97; www.pancakes. amsterdam; Berenstraat 38; mains €6-10.50; ⊙9am-6pm; ☎ ✎ ♿; ☐13/14/17 Westermarkt)

Drinking

't Smalle

BROWN CAFE

19 ☐ Map p48, C4

Dating back to 1786 as a *jenever* (Dutch gin) distillery and tasting house, and restored during the 1970s with antique porcelain beer pumps and lead-framed windows, locals' favourite 't Smalle is one of Amsterdam's most charming *bruin cafés* (traditional pubs). Dock your boat right by the pretty stone terrace, which is wonderfully convivial by day and impossibly romantic at night. (www. t-smalle.nl; Egelantiersgracht 12; ⊙10am-1am Sun-Thu, to 2am Fri & Sat; ☐13/14/17 Westermarkt)

Local Life

Drink Like a Jordaanian

There's a certain hard-drinking, hard-living spirit left over from the Jordaan's working-class days, when the neighbourhood burst with 80,000 residents (compared to today's 20,000) and brown cafes (bars) functioned as a refuge from the slings and arrows of work-aday life. Local bastions that are still going strong include **De Twee Zwaantjes** (Map p48, C4; ☏020-625 27 29; www.cafedetweezwaantjes.nl; Prinsengracht 114; ◷3pm-1am Sun-Thu, to 3am Fri & Sat; ◪13/14/17 Westermarkt), where patrons belt out classics and traditional Dutch tunes in a rollicking, unforgettable cabaret-meets-karaoke evening, and **Café de Jordaan** (Map p48, C7; ☏020-627 58 63; Elandsgracht 45; ◷10am-1am Mon-Thu, 10am-3am Fri, noon-3am Sat, 1pm-1am Sun; ◪7/10/17 Elandsgracht), which comes into its own at 5pm on Sunday, when crooners link arms and sing along to classic Dutch tunes.

't Arendsnest   BROWN CAFE

20 Map p48, D4

This gorgeous restyled *bruin café*, with its glowing copper *jenever* (Dutch gin) boilers behind the bar, only serves Dutch beer – but with over 100 varieties (many from small breweries), including 52 rotating on tap, you'll need to move here to try them all. It also has more than 40 gins, ciders, whiskies and liqueurs, all of which are Dutch too. (www.arendsnest.nl; Herengracht 90; ◷noon-midnight Sun-Thu, to 2am Fri & Sat; ◪1/2/5/13/17 Nieuwezijds Kolk)

Vesper Bar   COCKTAIL BAR

21 Map p48, D2

This luxe bar's location on a low-key stretch of Jordaanian shops and businesses gives it a certain mystique. Its martinis will coax out your inner James Bond – or Vesper Lynd (the main female character in *Casino Royale*). Spice things up with the Victoria's Secret: ginger liqueur, pear brandy and elderflower with fresh lemon juice and a dash of chilli pepper. (☏020-420 45 92; www.vesperbar.nl; Vinkenstraat 57; ◷8pm-1am Tue-Thu, 5pm-3am Fri & Sat; ◪18/21/22 Buiten Oranjestraat)

Cafe Soundgarden   BAR

22 Map p48, A5

In this grungy, all-ages dive bar, the 'Old Masters' are the Ramones and Black Sabbath. Somehow a handful of pool tables, 1980s pinball machines, unkempt DJs and lovably surly bartenders add up to an ineffable magic. Bands occasionally make an appearance, and the waterfront terrace scene is more like an impromptu party in someone's backyard. (www.cafesoundgarden.nl; Marnixstraat 164-166; ◷1pm-1am Mon-Thu, to 3am Fri, 3pm-3am Sat, to 1am Sun; ◪13/14/17 Marnixstraat)

Café Pieper   BROWN CAFE

23 🚇 Map p48, C8

Small, unassuming and unmistak-ably old (1665), Café Pieper features stained-glass windows, antique beer mugs hanging from the bar and a working Belgian beer pump (1875). Sip an Amsterdam-brewed Brouwerij 't IJ beer or a terrific cappuccino as you marvel at the claustrophobia of the low-ceilinged bar (people were shorter back in the 17th century – even the Dutch, it seems). (www.cafepieper.com; Prinsengracht 424; ⏰noon-1am Mon, Wed & Thu, 4pm-midnight Tue, noon-2am Fri & Sat, 2-10pm Sun; 🚊1/2/5 Prinsengracht)

Café Papeneiland   BROWN CAFE

24 🚇 Map p48, D2

With Delft-blue tiles and a central stove, this *bruin café* is a 1642 gem. The name, 'Papists' Island', goes back to the Reformation, when there was a clandestine Catholic church on the canal's northern side. Papeneiland was reached via a secret tunnel from the top of the stairs – ask the bar staff to show you the entrance. (www.papenei land.nl; Prinsengracht 2; ⏰10am-1am Sun-Thu, to 3am Fri & Sat; 🚊3/10 Marnixplein)

Struik   BAR

25 🚇 Map p48, B5

If you prefer your beer with a background of hip hop, breakbeats and soul, come to this graffitied, split-level corner *café* with a spinning disco ball above the entrance, where the neighbourhood's hipsters linger drinking and chatting as the candles wear down. Guest chefs whip up inexpensive meals on various nights. Cash only. (Rozengracht 160; ⏰5pm-1am Sun-Thu, to 3am Fri & Sat; 🚊13/14/17 Marnixstraat)

Understand
Gezelligheid

- -

This particularly Dutch quality is one of the best reasons to visit Amsterdam. It's variously translated as snug, friendly, cosy, informal, companionable and convivial, but *gezelligheid* – the state of being *gezellig* – is something more easily experienced than defined. There's a sense of time stopping, an intimacy of the here and now that leaves all your troubles behind, at least until tomorrow. You can get the warm and fuzzy feeling in many places and situations: while nursing a brew with friends, over coffee and cake with neighbours, or lingering after a meal (the Dutch call this *natafelen*, or 'after-table-ing'). Nearly any cosy establishment lit by candles probably qualifies. Old brown cafes, such as 't Smalle (p55) and Café Pieper, practically have *gezelligheid* on tap.

Local Life

Neighbourhood Markets

The **Lindengracht Market** (Map p48, C2; www.jordaanmarkten.nl; Lindengracht; ⏱9am-4pm Sat; 🚊3 Nieuwe Willemsstraat) is a wonderfully authentic local affair, with bountiful fresh produce, including fish and magnificent cheese stalls, as well as gourmet goods, clothing and homewares. Arrive as early as possible for the best pickings and smallest crowds.

Another good one for treasure hunters is the **Westermarkt** (Map p48, C5; www.jordaanmarkten.nl; Westerstraat; ⏱9am-1pm Mon; 🚊3/10 Marnixplein), where bargain-priced clothing and fabrics are sold at 170 stalls; note it isn't in fact on Westerstraat but on Westerstraat, just near the Noordermarkt.

Café P 96 BROWN CAFE

26 Map p48, C4

If you don't want the night to end, P 96 is an amiable hang-out. When most other *cafés* in the Jordaan shut down for the night, this is where everyone ends up, rehashing their evening and striking up conversations with strangers. In summertime head to the terrace across the street aboard a houseboat. (http://p96.nl; Prinsengracht 96; ⏱11am-3am Sun-Thu, to 4am Fri & Sat; 🛜; 🚊13/14/17 Westermarkt)

De Trut GAY & LESBIAN

27 Map p48, A8

In the basement of a former squat, this Sunday-night club is a gay and lesbian institution. It's run by volunteers and comes with an attitude; arrive well before 11pm (the space is fairly small). No cameras and no mobile phones are allowed inside. (www.trutfonds.nl; Bilderdijkstraat 165e; ⏱10pm-4am Sun; 🚊7/17 Bilderdijkstraat)

Entertainment

Boom Chicago COMEDY

28 ⭐ Map p48, B5

Boom Chicago stages seriously funny improv-style comedy shows in English that make fun of Dutch culture, American culture and everything that gets in the cross-hairs. Edgier shows happen in the smaller upstairs theatre. The on-site bar helps fuel the festivities with buckets of ice and beer. (www.boomchicago.nl; Rozengracht 117; tickets from €15; 🛜; 🚊13/14/17 Marnixstraat)

De Nieuwe Anita LIVE MUSIC

29 ⭐ Map p48, A5

This living-room venue expanded for noise rockers has a great *café*. Behind the bookcase-concealed door, in the back, the main room has a stage and screens cult movies (in English) on Monday. DJs and vaudeville-type acts are also on the eclectic agenda. (www.denieuweanita.nl; Frederik Hendrikstraat 111; tickets free-€5; 🚊3 Hugo de Grootplein)

Understand

Canals

History

In Dutch a canal is a *gracht* (pronounced 'khrakht'), and the main canals form the central *grachtengordel* (canal ring). These beauties came to life in the early 1600s, after Amsterdam outgrew its medieval walls and city planners put together an ambitious design for expansion. Far from being simply picturesque, or even just waterways for transport, the canals were needed to drain and reclaim the waterlogged land. In 2010 Unesco declared the 400-year-old waterways a World Heritage site.

Core Canals

Starting from the core, the major semicircular canals are the Singel, Herengracht, Keizersgracht and Prinsengracht. An easy way to remember them is that, apart from the **Singel** (originally a moat that defended Amsterdam's outer limits), these canals are in alphabetical order. The **Herengracht** is where Amsterdam's wealthiest residents moved once the canals were completed. They named the waterway after the Heeren XVII (17 Gentlemen) of the Dutch East India Company, and built their mansions alongside it. Almost as swanky was the **Keizersgracht** (Emperor's Canal), a nod to Holy Roman Emperor Maximilian I. The **Prinsengracht** – named after William the Silent, Prince of Orange and the first Dutch royal – was designed as a slightly cheaper canal with smaller residences and warehouses. It also acted as a barrier against the crusty working-class quarter beyond, aka the Jordaan. Today the Prinsengracht is the liveliest of Amsterdam's inner canals, with *cafés*, shops and houseboats lining the quays.

Radial Canals

The three major radial canals cut across the core canals like spokes on a bicycle. The **Brouwersgracht** – aka the 'Brewers Canal' – is one of Amsterdam's most beautiful waterways. It takes its name from the many breweries that lined the banks in the 16th and 17th centuries. The **Leidsegracht** was named after the city of Leiden, to which it was the main water route. Peaceful **Reguliersgracht** was named after an order of monks whose monastery was located nearby.

Movies

CINEMA

30 ⭐ Map p48, C1

Amsterdam's oldest cinema, dating from 1912, is a *gezellig* (cosy) gem screening indie films alongside mainstream flicks. From Sunday to Thursday you can treat yourself to a meal in the restaurant (open 5.30pm to 10pm) or have a pre-film tipple at the inviting *café*-bar. (☎020-638 60 16; www.themovies.nl; Haarlemmerdijk 161; tickets €11; 🚊3 Haarlemmerplein)

Maloe Melo

BLUES

31 ⭐ Map p48, B7

This is the freewheeling, fun-loving altar of Amsterdam's tiny blues scene.

Understand
Liquorice

The Dutch love their sweets, the most famous of which is *drop,* the word for all varieties of liquorice. It may be gummy-soft or tough as leather, and shaped like coins or miniature cars, but the most important distinction is between *zoete* (sweet) and *zoute* (salty, also called *salmiak*). The latter is often an alarming surprise, even for avowed fans of the black stuff. But with such a range of textures and additional flavours – mint, honey, laurel – even liquorice sceptics might be converted. Het Oud-Hollandsch Snoepwinkeltje is a good place to do a taste test.

Music ranges from funk and soul to Texas blues and rockabilly. The cover charge is usually around €5. (☎020-420 45 92; www.maloemelo.com; Lijnbaansgracht 163; ⏰9pm-3am Sun-Thu, to 4am Fri & Sat; 🚊7/10/17 Elandsgracht)

Shopping

Frozen Fountain

HOMEWARES

32 🔒 Map p48, C7

Frozen Fountain is Amsterdam's best-known showcase of furniture and interior design. Prices are not cheap, but the daring designs are offbeat and very memorable (designer penknives, kitchen gadgets and that birthday gift for the impossible-to-wow friend). Best of all, it's an unpretentious place where you can browse at length without feeling uncomfortable. (www.frozenfountain.nl; Prinsengracht 645; ⏰1-6pm Mon, 10am-6pm Tue-Sat, noon-5pm Sun; 🚊1/2/5 Prinsengracht)

De Kaaskamer

FOOD

42 🔒 Map p48

The name means 'the cheese room' and De Kaaskamer is indeed stacked to the rafters with Dutch and organic varieties, as well as olives, tapenades, salads and other picnic ingredients. You can try before you buy or pick up a cheese-filled baguette. Vacuum packing is available to take cheeses home. (www.kaaskamer.nl; Runstraat 7; ⏰noon-6pm Mon, 9am-6pm Tue-Fri, 9am-5pm Sat, noon-5pm Sun; 🚊1/2/5 Spui)

Keizersgracht (p59)

Moooi Gallery

DESIGN

33 Map p48, C3

Founded by Marcel Wanders, this gallery-shop features Dutch design at its most over-the-top, from the life-size black horse lamp to the 'blow away vase' (a whimsical twist on the classic Delft vase) and the 'killing of the piggy bank' ceramic pig (with a gold hammer). (☎020-528 77 60; www. moooi.com; Westerstraat 187; ⏱10am-6pm Tue-Sat; 🚊3/10 Marnixplein)

Marie-Stella-Maris

COSMETICS

34 Map p48, D7

Set up as a social enterprise to provide clean drinking water worldwide, Marie-Stella-Maris donates a percentage from every purchase of its locally bottled mineral waters and its aromatic plant-based skincare products (body lotions, hand soaps, shea butter) and home fragrances (from travel-pillow sprays to scented candles) to support its cause. Its basement cafe–water bar opens at weekends. (www.marie-stella-maris.com; Keizersgracht 357; ⏱10am-6pm Tue-Sat, noon-6pm Sun & Mon; 🚊1/2/5 Keizersgracht)

Het Oud-Hollandsch Snoepwinkeltje

FOOD

35 Map p48, C4

This corner shop is lined with jar after apothecary jar of Dutch penny sweets with flavours from chocolate to coffee, all manner of fruit and the salty Dutch liquorice known as *drop*. It also stocks diabetic-friendly sweets. (www.snoepwinkeltje.com; 2e Egelantiersdwarsstraat 2; ⏱11am-6.30pm Tue-Sat; 🚊3/10 Marnixplein)

Robins Hood   DESIGN

36 Map p48, C4

Whitewashed walls and floorboards create a blank canvas for the sustainably produced upcycled vintage and Dutch-designed products here. Browse for unique items like vases, bags, scarves, jewellery, sunglasses, lamps, art, stationery and some truly only-in-the-Netherlands items like

stroopwafel coasters. (www.robinshood.nl; 2e Tuindwarsstraat 7; ⏱11am-6pm Mon-Fri, to 5pm Sat; 🚊3/10 Marnixplein)

Mechanisch Speelgoed   TOYS

37 Map p48, C3

This adorable shop is crammed full of nostalgic toys, including snow domes, glow lamps, masks, finger puppets and wind-up toys. And who doesn't need a good rubber chicken every once in a while? Hours can vary. (http://mechanisch-speelgoed.nl; Westerstraat 67; ⏱10am-6pm Mon-Fri, to 5pm Sat; 🚊3/10 Marnixplein)

Galleria d'Arte Rinascimento   ART, ANTIQUES

38 Map p48, C5

Royal Delftware ceramics (both antique and new) at this pretty shop span all manner of vases, platters, brooches, Christmas ornaments and intriguing 19th-century wall tiles and plaques. (☎020-622 75 09; www.delft-art-gallery.com; Prinsengracht 170; ⏱9am-6pm; 🚊13/14/17 Westermarkt)

't Zonnetje   DRINKS

39 Map p48, D2

At this charming shop ensconced in a 1642 building, you can find teas from all over the world, as well as coffees, spices and accoutrements. (☎020-623 00 58; www.t-zonnetje.com; Haarlemmerdijk 45; ⏱9-6pm Mon-Fri, to 5pm Sat; 🚊18/21/22 Buiten Oranjestraat)

De Kaaskamer (p60)

I Love Vintage

VINTAGE

40 🔒 Map p48, D4

A large shop compared to most Amsterdam vintage purveyors, I Love Vintage has a terrific selection of dresses and jewellery from the 1920s to the 1950s. If preworn threads aren't your thing, it also carries retro-style new clothes. (www.ilovevintage.com; Prinsengracht 201; ⊙10am-7pm Mon-Sat, noon-5pm Sun; 🚊13/14/17 Westermarkt)

360 Volt

HOMEWARES

41 🔒 Map p48, C6

One of the keys to creating a quintessentially *gezellig* (cosy, convivial) atmosphere is ambient lighting, making this shop stocking vintage industrial lighting (restored to meet energy-efficient international standards) a real find. Its lights grace some of the world's hottest bars, restaurants, hotels and film sets, such as the James Bond instalment *Spectre*. Worldwide shipping can be arranged. (☑020-810 01 01; https://360volt.com; Prinsengracht 397; ⊙11am-6pm Thu-Sat, by appointment Tue & Wed; 🚊13/14/17 Westermarkt)

Local Life
Westerpark & Western Islands

Getting There

The area borders the Jordaan to the north-west; it's 1.6km from Centraal Station.

Tram 3 and 10 swing by the area.

Bus 22 goes to Het Schip.

A reedy wilderness, a post-industrial culture complex and a drawbridge-filled adventure await those who make the trip to Westerpark and the Western Islands. Architectural and foodie hotspots add to the hip, eco-urban mash-up. The area's rags-to-riches story is prototypical Amsterdam: abandoned factoryland hits the skids, squatters salvage it, and it rises again in creative fashion.

❶ Architecture

The remarkable housing project **Het Schip** (☎020-686 85 95; www.hetschip.nl; Oostzaanstraat 45; tour adult/child €12.50/free; ⏰11am-5pm Tue-Sun, English tour 3pm; 🚊22 Oostzaanstraat) is the pinnacle of Amsterdam School architecture. Michel de Klerk designed the triangular block, loosely resembling a ship, for railway employees. There is a small museum where you can see the old post office and an apartment.

❷ Patch of Green

From Het Schip, walk southeast along the train tracks and cut through an underpass to **Westerpark** (Spaarndammerstraat; 🚊3 Haarlemmerplein). The pond-dappled green space is a cool-cat hang-out that blends into Westergasfabriek, a former gasworks transformed into an edgy cultural park, whose buildings hold *cafés*, theatres, breweries and other creative spaces.

❸ Terrace Drinks

On sunny afternoons young, artsy professionals flock to the massive decked outdoor terrace at **Westergasterras** (www.westergasterras.nl; Klönneplein 4-6, Westergasfabriek; ⏰11am-1am Mon-Thu, to 3am Fri, 10am-3am Sat, to 1am Sun; 🛜; 🚊10 Van Limburg Stirumstraat). A toasty fireplace makes the cafe equally inviting indoors. It's perfect for a vino and mackerel salad sandwich. Late at night on weekends it morphs into a club.

❹ Mussels & Gin

Mosselen (mussels) and gin are the twin specialities of spectacular double-height mezzanine space **Mossel En Gin** (☎020-486 58 69; www.mosselengin.nl; Gosschalklaan 12, Westergasfabriek; mains €12-16; ⏰4-10pm Tue-Fri, 1-10pm Sat & Sun, bar to 1am Tue-Thu & Sun, to 3am Fri & Sat; 🛜; 🚊21 Van Hallstraat), which opens to two sun-soaked beer gardens. Mussels-and-fries come in four styles, including with crème fraîche and gin; it also serves inspired gin-and-tonic-battered fish and chips, and lobster or shrimp croquettes with gin mayo. Alongside seven gins, six house infusions include beetroot and basil.

❺ Western Islands

The **Western Islands** were originally home to shipworks and the Dutch West India Company's warehouses, which buzzed with activity in the early 1600s. The district is a world unto itself, cut through with canals and linked with small drawbridges. It's well worth a wander among the charming homes and artist studios.

❻ Scenic Zandhoek

Visit photogenic **Zandhoek** (Realeneiland; 🚊48 Barentszplein), a stretch of waterfront on the eastern shore. Now a yacht harbour, back in the 17th century it was a 'sand market', where ships would purchase bags of the stuff for ballast.

❼ Foodie Love at Marius

Foodies swoon over pocket-sized **Marius** (☎020-422 78 80; http://restaurantmarius.nl; Barentszstraat 173; 4-course menu €47.50; ⏰6.30-10pm Tue-Sat; 🚊3 Zoutkeetsgracht). Chef Kees shops daily at local markets.The result might be grilled prawns with fava bean purée or beef rib with polenta and ratatouille.

Explore

Southern Canal Ring

This horseshoe-shaped loop of parallel canals is home to the nightlife hubs of Leidseplein and Rembrandtplein, with bars, clubs and restaurants clustered around large squares. Between these two districts, the canals are lined by some of the city's most elegant houses; the area also encompasses many fine museums, a flower market and waterside restaurants and bars.

The Sights in a Day

☀ Devote the morning to whatever mega art exhibit the **Hermitage Amsterdam** (p72; pictured left) is showing. Then stroll over to the **Tassenmuseum Hendrikje** (p74), a museum dedicated to handbags and purses throughout history inside a Golden Age canal house.

☀ Begin the afternoon at Rembrandtplein and do the tourist thing. Snap a photo with the master painter's statue, eat a *kroket* (croquette) at **Van Dobben** (p74) and finish with a drink at splendid, velvet-chaired **De Kroon** (p80). Next saunter over to **Museum Van Loon** (p72) for a look at the moneyed canal-house lifestyle, and to **Foam** (p72) for renowned photography exhibits.

☾ For dinner, choose one of the smart bars and restaurants along Utrechtsestraat – maybe **Tempo Doeloe** (p76) for Indonesian or **Bar Moustache** (p77) for Italian. You'll need a solid meal to energise the evening's activities around Leidseplein. See what's on at **Paradiso** (p81), **Melkweg** (p81) and **Jazz Café Alto** (p82). Prefer something more laid-back? Try beery **Eijlders** (p79).

For a local's day in the Southern Canal Ring, see p68.

○ Local Life

Strolling the Southern Canal Ring (p68)

♥ Best of Amsterdam

Best Canals

Golden Bend (p69)

Reguliersgracht (p82)

Buffet van Odette (p74)

Best Shopping

Mobilia (p83)

Young Designers United (p82)

Bloemenmarkt (p68)

Best Entertainment

Melkweg (p81)

Paradiso (p81)

Stadsschouwburg (p69)

Pathé Tuschinskitheater (p80)

Getting There

🚊 **Tram** The neighbourhood is well-served by trams. For the Leidseplein area, take tram 1, 2, 5, 7 or 10. To reach Rembrandtplein, take tram 4, which travels down Utrechtsestraat, or tram 9. Trams 16 and 24 cut through the centre of the neighbourhood down busy Vijzelstraat.

Local Life
Strolling the Southern Canal Ring

Puttin' on the Ritz is nothing new to the Southern Canal Belt. Most of the area was built at the end of the 17th century, when Amsterdam was wallowing in Golden Age cash. A wander through reveals grand mansions, swanky antique shops, an indulgent patisserie and a one-of-a-kind kitty museum. And while it's all stately, it's certainly not snobby.

1 **Flower Market**

The canalside **Bloemenmarkt** (Flower Market; Singel, btwn Muntplein & Konings-plein; ⏱8.30am-7pm Mon-Sat, to 7.30pm Sun Apr-Oct, 9am-5.30pm Mon-Sat, 11am-5.30pm Sun Nov-Mar; 🚃1/2/5 Koningsplein) has been here since 1860. Exotic bulbs are the main stock, though cut flowers brighten the stalls, too. Buy a bouquet: there's no better way to feel like a local than walking around with flowers in the crook of your arm.

❷ Golden Bend Riches

During the Golden Age, the **Golden Bend** (Gouden Bocht; Herengracht, btwn Leidsestraat & Vijzelstraat; 🚊1/2/5 Koningsplein) was the 'it' spot, where the wealthiest Amsterdammers lived, loved and ruled their affairs. Look up at the mansions as you walk along the Herengracht. Many date from the 1660s. The gables here were allowed to be twice as wide as the standard Amsterdam model.

❸ Odd art at the Kattenkabinet

The only Golden Bend abode that's open to the public is the **Kattenkabinet** (Cat Cabinet; 📞020-626 90 40; www.kattenkabinet.nl; Herengracht 497; adult/child €7/free; 🕙10am-5pm Mon-Fri, from noon Sat & Sun; 🚊1/2/5 Koningsplein), an offbeat museum devoted to cat-related art. A Picasso drawing, kitschy kitty lithographs and odd pieces of ephemera cram the creaky old house. Happy live felines lounge on the window seats.

❹ Treats at Patisserie Holtkamp

When you arrive at **Patisserie Holtkamp** (www.patisserieholtkamp.nl; Vijzelgracht 15; dishes €3-6.50; 🕙8.30am-6pm Mon-Fri, to 5pm Sat; 🚊4/7/10/16/24 Weteringcircuit), look up to spot the gilded royal coat of arms, topped by a crown, attached to the brick facade: this swanky bakery supplies the Dutch royals with delicacies including *kroketten* (croquets) with fillings of prawns, lobster and veal.

❺ Spiegel Quarter Antiques

When it's time to decorate that mansion, folks head to the long line of shops along Spiegelgracht and Nieuwe Spiegelstraat, aka the **Spiegel Quarter**. The perfect Delft vase or 16th-century wall map will most assuredly be hiding among the antique stores, bric-a-brac shops and commercial art galleries.

❻ Theatre Time

The neo-Renaissance **Stadsschouwburg** (📞020-624 23 11; www.stadsschouwburgamsterdam.nl; Leidseplein 26; 🕙box office noon-6pm Mon-Sat; 🚊1/2/5/7/10 Leidseplein) takes pride of place on the Leidseplein. The regal venue, built in 1894, is used for large-scale plays, operettas and the Holland Festival, the country's biggest music, drama and arts extravaganza. Amsterdam's main ticket desk, where you can get seats for shows around town, is also stashed inside.

❼ Drinks at Café Americain

Pull up a chair, order a cappuccino and watch the world spin by at **Café Americain** (📞020-556 30 10; www.cafeamericain.nl; Leidsekade 97, Amsterdam American Hotel; 🕙5.30am-midnight; 🚊1/2/5/7/10 Leidseplein). The art-nouveau monument, opened in 1902, was a *grand café* before the concept even existed, with huge stained-glass windows overlooking Leidseplein, a lovely, library-like reading table and a great terrace.

A **B** **C** **D**

1

Passeerdersgr

Prinsengr

Prinsengr

Molenpad

Leidsegr

Leidsegracht

Keizersgr

40

Keizersgr

Singel

P Raamstr

P

Lijnbaansgr

7.10

Leidsegr

Keizersgr

Leidsestr

11
Kerkstr

1.2.5

Leidsestr

Keizersgracht

23

Herengr

Herengracht

Herengr

19

24

14

2

Marnixstr

Lijnbaansgr

38

35

27
Korte Leidsedwarsstr

Leidsestr

Amsterdam
Pipe Museum
5

Prinsengr

Prinsengracht

Nieuwe Spiegelstr

Leidseplein

Leidsedwarsstr

25

26

37 13

12

33

Leidsekruisstr

Lange Leidsedwarsstr

Prinsengr

42

Kerkstr

3

Leidsebosje

Hirschpassage

Max
Euweplein

36

Leidsekade

Ziesenliskade

Lijnbaansgr

Weteringschans

Spiegelgr

9

Weteringstr

2e Weteringdwars

3e Weteringdwarst

10

Nieuwe Weteringst

Lijnbaansgracht

4

P

Zandpad

Vossiusstr

Pieter Cornelisz Hooftstr

Hobbemastr

Singelgracht

Stadhouderskade

Jan Luijkenstr

Rijksmuseum

Paulus Potterstr

2.5

Hobbemakade

Boerenwetering

5

N 0 —————— 200 m
0 —————— 0.1 miles

E
Singel
Muntplein

F
Korte
Reguliers-
dwarsstr
Reguliersbreestr
Halvemaan-
steeg
Binnen Amstel

G
Amstel

H
Stopera
Waterlooplein

29
Reguliersdwarsstr

34
32
31
16
Bakkerstr
Paardenstr
Wagenstr

Blauwbrug

Golden
Bend
20
8
30
Rembrandtplein
Amstelstr 22

Museum Willet-
Holthuysen
4

Hermitage
Amsterdam
1

Vijzelstr

Tassenmuseum
Hendrikje
7
Herengr
Thorbeckeplein

Herengracht

Herengr

Utrechtsestr
Amstel

Stadsarchief
6

Foam
3
Keizersgr

Keizersgr
Keizersgracht
Keizersgr

Keizersgr

Magere
Brug

2
Museum
Van Loon

39
43
18
4
Kerkstr

16, 24

Prinsengr

Prinsengr
Amstelveld

Utrechtsestr
Prinsengracht
Prinsengracht

41

17
Prinsengr

Noorderstr

Utrechtsedwarsstr
21
28

Achtergr

Vijzelgr

Nieuwe Looiersstr

Fokke Simonszstr

Reguliersgracht

15
Falckstr

Frederiksplein

Sarphatistr

Weteringschans

Wetering-
circuit

Den Texstr

Nicolaas Witsenstr

Nicolaas Witsenkade

For reviews see

⊙	Sights	p72
⊗	Eating	p74
⊕	Drinking	p77
✿	Entertainment	p80
⊕	Shopping	p82

Sights

Hermitage Amsterdam   MUSEUM

1 Map p70, H2

There have long been links between Russia and the Netherlands – Tsar Peter the Great learned shipbuilding here in 1697 – hence this branch of St Petersburg's State Hermitage Museum. Blockbuster temporary exhibitions show works from the Hermitage, while the permanent *Portrait Gallery of the Golden Age* has formal group portraits of the 17th-century Dutch A-list; the Outsider Gallery also has temporary shows. I Amsterdam and Museum cards allow free entrance or a discount, depending on the exhibition. (☑020-530 74 88; www.hermitage.nl; Amstel 51; single exhibitions adult/child €17.50/free, all exhibitions adult/child €25/free; ⏱10am-5pm; Ⓜ Waterlooplein, 🚊9/14 Waterlooplein)

Museum Van Loon   MUSEUM

2 Map p70, E3

An insight into life at the top of the pile in the 19th century, Museum Van Loon is an opulent 1672 residence that was first home to painter Ferdinand Bol and later to the wealthy Van Loon family. Important paintings such as *The Marriage of Willem van Loon and Margaretha Bas* by Jan Miense Molenaer and a collection of some 150 portraits hang inside sumptuous interiors. (☑020-624 52 55; www.museumvanloon.nl; Keizersgracht 672; adult/child €9/5, free with Museum & I Amsterdam cards; ⏱10am-5pm; 🚊16/24 Keizersgracht)

Foam   GALLERY

3 Map p70, E2

From the outside it looks like a grand canal house, but this is the city's most important photography gallery. Its simple, spacious galleries, some with skylights or large windows for natural light, host four major exhibitions annually, featuring world-renowned photographers such as William Eggleston and Helmut Newton. There's a **cafe** in the basement. (Fotografiemuseum Amsterdam; www.foam.org; Keizersgracht 609; adult/child €11/free; ⏱10am-6pm Sat-Wed, to 9pm Thu & Fri; 🚊16/24 Keizersgracht)

Museum Willet-Holthuysen   MUSEUM

4 Map p70, G2

This exquisite canal house was built in 1687 for Amsterdam mayor Jacob Hop, then remodelled in 1739. It's named after Louisa Willet-Holthuysen, who inherited the house from her coal-and-glass-merchant father and lived a lavish, bohemian life here with her husband. She bequeathed the property to the city in 1895. With displays including part of the family's 275-piece Meissen table service, and an immaculate French-style garden, the museum is a fascinating window into the 19th-century world of the super-rich. (☑020-523 18 22; www.willetholthuysen.nl; Herengracht 605; adult/child €9/4.50, free with Museum & I Amsterdam cards, audioguide €1; ⏱10am-5pm Mon-Fri, from 11am Sat & Sun; Ⓜ Waterlooplein, 🚊4/9/14 Rembrandtplein)

Museum Van Loon

Amsterdam Pipe Museum

MUSEUM

5 Map p70, B2

This museum is located in the grand 17th-century canal house of the single-minded pipe collector who gathered this unexpectedly fascinating collection from around 60 different countries over 40 years. Knowledgeable guides take you through the exhibits, from the earliest South American pipes, dating from 500 BC, to 15th-century Dutch pipes, Chinese opium pipes, African ceremonial pipes and much more. A peek into the house is worth the price of admission alone. (www.pipemuseum.nl; Prinsengracht 488; adult/child €8/4; ☺noon-6pm Wed-Sat; 🚊1/2/5 Prinsengracht)

Stadsarchief

MUSEUM

6 Map p70, E2

A distinctive striped building dating from 1923, this former bank houses 23km of shelving storing Amsterdam archives. Fascinating displays of archive gems, such as the 1942 police report on the theft of Anne Frank's bike and a letter from Charles Darwin to Artis Royal Zoo in 1868, can be viewed in the tiled basement vault. Tours (1¼ hours) run at 2pm on Saturday and Sunday, and must be booked in advance. (Municipal Archives; ☎020-251 15 11, tour reservations 020-251 15 10; www.amsterdam.nl/stadsarchief; Vijzelstraat 32; admission free, tours adult/child €6/free; ☺10am-5pm Tue-Fri, from noon Sat & Sun; 🚊16/24 Keizersgracht)

Tassenmuseum Hendrikje

MUSEUM

7 ◉ Map p70, F2

This grand 17th-century canal house museum has a covetable collection of more than 5000 bags, including a medieval pouch, 1960s Perspex containers, design classics by Chanel, Gucci and Versace, an '80s touch-tone phone bag and Madonna's ivy-strewn 'Evita' bag from the film's premiere. The **cafe** has pricey-but-nice high teas and cakes. (Museum of Bags & Purses; ☎020-524 64 52; www.tassenmuseum.nl; Herengracht 573; adult/child €12.50/3.50; ⊙10am-5pm; 🚊4/9/14 Rembrandtplein)

Eating

Van Dobben

DUTCH €

8 ✗ Map p70, F1

Open since the 1940s, Van Dobben has a cool diner feel, with white tiles and siren-red walls. Traditional meaty Dutch fare is its forte: low-priced, finely sliced roast-beef sandwiches with mustard are an old-fashioned joy, or try the *pekelvlees* (akin to corned beef) or *halfom* (if you're keen on *pekelvlees* mixed with liver). (☎020-624 42 00; www.eetsalonvandobben.nl; Korte Reguliersdwarsstraat 5-9; dishes €3-8; ⊙10am-9pm Mon-Wed, to 1am Thu, to 2am Fri & Sat, 10.30am-8pm Sun; 🚊4/9/14 Rembrandtplein)

Buffet van Odette

CAFE €€

9 ✗ Map p70, D3

Chow down at Odette's, a white-tiled cafe with an enchanting canalside spot, where delicious dishes are made with great ingredients and a dash of creativity. Try the splendid platter of cured meats and dips, or mains such as ravioli with mature cheese, watercress and tomato, or smoked salmon, lentils and poached egg. (☎020-423 60 34; www.buffetvanodette.nl; Prinsengracht 598; mains €13.50-18.50; ⊙kitchen 10am-10pm; 🚊7/10 Spiegelgracht)

La Cacerola

SPANISH €€

10 ✗ Map p70, D4

Open since 1958, this romantic gem serves up gourmet meals prepared according to Slow Food principles. Try the chef's surprise four-course menu, or, if you like to know what you're going to eat, go a la carte, with hearty dishes such as rack of lamb with Mediterranean vegetables and potato ratatouille. (☎020-627 93 97; www.restaurantlacacerola.nl; Weteringstraat 41; mains €18.50-25; ⊙6-10.30pm Tue-Sat; 🚊7/10 Spiegelgracht)

Local Life

Utrechtsestraat

A stone's throw south from gaudy Rembrandtplein, Utrechtsestraat is a relaxed artery stocked with enticing shops, designer bars and cosy eateries – a prime place to wander and discover a great local hangout. The street's southern end used to terminate at the Utrechtse Poort, a gate to the nearby city of Utrecht, hence the name.

Ron Gastrobar Oriental ASIAN €€

11 Map p70, B1

Michelin-starred chef Ron Blaauw began his food revolution at Ron Gastrobar (p99) near Vondelpark, introducing a one-price menu of tapas-style dishes so diners could eat fine cuisine without settling down for a long formal meal. This is his Asian version. The menu includes delicacies such as dim sum of steamed scallop with glass noodles, and crispy sweet and sour prawns. (☏020-223 53 52; www.rongastrobaroriental.nl; Kerkstraat 23; dim sum €2-9.50, mains €15; ⏱5.30-11pm; 🛜; 🚊1/2/5 Prinsengracht)

Pantry DUTCH €€

12 Map p70, B3

With wood-panelled walls and sepia lighting, this little restaurant is *gezellig* (cosy) indeed. Tuck into classic Dutch dishes such as *zuurkool stamppot* (sauerkraut and potato mash served with a smoked sausage or meatball) or *hutspot* ('hotchpotch', with stewed beef, carrots and onions). (☏020-620 09 22; www.thepantry.nl; Leidsekruisstraat 21; mains €13-18, 3-course menus €21-30; ⏱11am-10.30pm; 🚊1/2/5 Leidseplein)

De Blauwe Hollander DUTCH €€

13 Map p70, B3

It's all cosiness and comfort food at this red-lamp-lit place, with a menu including Dutch staples such as pea soup with bacon, and *stamppot* (veggie mash) with pork sausage. Look

for the Dutch flag flying out front. (☏020-627 05 21; www.deblauwehollander.nl; Leidsekruisstraat 28; mains €13.75-19.50; ⏱noon-11pm; 🚊1/2/5 Leidseplein)

Rose's Cantina MEXICAN €€

14 Map p70, D1

Rose's has a grass-green interior topped by massive glitter balls, and a greenery-fringed courtyard. Both are great settings for enjoying starters such as ceviche (raw fish cured in lime juice) and Mexican mains with a twist, such as pulled-pork or crab tacos, black bean–filled enchiladas with sour cream, and spicy sweet-potato empanadas with chipotle mayo and salsa. (☏020-625 97 97; www.rosescantina.com;

Reguliersdwarsstraat 38-48; mains €16.50-24; ⏱5.30-10.30pm; 📶; 🚊1/2/5 Koningsplein)

Bouchon du Centre FRENCH €€

15 Map p70, G4

Classic red-and-white gingham tablecloths set the scene at this authentic-feeling Lyonnais *bouchon* (informal rustic bistro). The menu changes daily, but revolves around *bouchon* staples such as *andouillette* (offal sausage) and *quenelles de brochet* (pike dumplings). Don't miss a round of wonderfully gooey St Marcellin cheese and Rhône Valley wines such as Beaujolais. (📱020-330 11 28; www.bouchonducentre.nl; Falckstraat 3; mains €15-20; ⏱noon-3pm & 5-8pm Wed-Sat; 🚊4/7/10 Frederiksplein)

Lo Stivale d'Oro ITALIAN €€

16 Map p70, H1

Conviviality is the name of the game at the 'Golden Boot', which offers a textbook gregarious Italian welcome, plus awesome pizzas and pastas. Italian owner Mario occasionally pulls out his guitar and strums for the crowd. (📱020-638 73 07; www.lostivale doro.nl; Amstelstraat 49; pizza €7.50-12.50, mains €8-22.50; ⏱5-10.30pm Wed-Mon; 🚊4/9/14 Rembrandtplein)

Piet de Leeuw STEAK €€

17 Map p70, E4

With its dark-wood furniture and wood-panelled walls hung with pictures, this feels like an old-school pub. The building dates from 1900, but it's been a steakhouse and a hang-out since the 1940s. Sit down at individual or communal tables and tuck into good-value steaks topped with a choice of sauces and served with salad and piping hot *frites* (French fries). (📱020-623 71 81; www.pietdeleeuw. nl; Noorderstraat 11; mains €12.75-22.50; ⏱noon-10.30pm Mon-Fri, from 5pm Sat & Sun; 🚊16/24 Keizersgracht)

Tempo Doeloe INDONESIAN €€€

18 Map p70, G3

Cosy Tempo Doeloe, with white tablecloths, chandeliers and draped curtains, is among Amsterdam's best, if *pittig* (spicy), Indonesian choices. It's recommended for a *rijsttafel* (Indonesian banquet) comprising 20-plus different concoctions. Warning: dishes marked 'very hot' are indeed like napalm. The wine list is excellent. (📱020-625 67 18; www.tempodoeloerestau rant.nl; Utrechtsestraat 75; mains around €35, rijsttafel & set menus €30-50; ⏱6-11.30pm Mon-Sat; 📶; 🚊4 Prinsengracht)

Bar Huf AMERICAN €

19 Map p70, D1

It can be hard to find good late-night dining in Amsterdam, but this place is a boon for nightbird burger lovers. Dig into the Mango Jerry (crab, coleslaw and wasabi mayo) or Rocky Balboa (chicken, jalapenos and cheddar) burgers, or try rum- and apple-glazed ribs or macaroni and cheese (made with five different cheeses). Finish with lemon meringue pie. (www.barhuf. nl; Reguliersdwarsstraat 43; mains €8.50-

Paradiso (p81)

14.50; ⊗kitchen 5pm-midnight Sun-Thu, to 1am Fri & Sat; 🔊; 🚊1/2/5 Koningsplein)

Drinking

Door 74   COCKTAIL BAR

 20 Map p70, E1

You'll need to leave a voice message or, better yet, send a text for a reservation to gain entry to this speakeasy behind an unmarked door. Some of Amsterdam's most amazing cocktails are served in a classy, dark-timbered Prohibition-era atmosphere beneath pressed-tin ceilings. Themed cocktail lists change regularly. Very cool. (🖉06 3404 5122; www.door-74.nl; Reguliersdwar-sstraat 74; ⊗8pm-3am Sun-Thu, to 4am Fri & Sat; 🚊9/14 Rembrandtplein)

Bar Moustache   BAR

21 Map p70, G4

Designed by lifestyle magazine editor Stella Willing, this loft-style, exposed-brick, New York-esque bar mixes up communal and private tables. It's a hot spot for hip locals, who make a beeline for the bar's window seats. Keeping everyone happily sated is the pared-down Italian menu and a great drink selection that includes Italian wines by the glass. (www.barmoustache.nl; Utrechtsestraat 141; ⊗8am-1am Mon-Thu, 9am-3am Fri & Sat, 9am-1am Sun; 🚊4 Prinsengracht)

SARAH COGHILL/LONELY PLANET ©

Air
CLUB

22 Map p70, G1

Big names like Pete Tong cut loose on the awesome sound system at it-club Air, which has interiors – including a tiered dance floor – by Dutch designer Marcel Wanders. Thoughtful touches include lockers and refillable cards that preclude fussing with change at the five bars. (www.air.nl; Amstelstraat 16; ⏰usually 11pm-4am Fri-Sun; 🚊4/9/14 Rembrandtplein)

The Otherside
COFFEESHOP

23 Map p70, D1

This buzzing choice has designer chandeliers and a lively, laid-back vibe. It's on the neighbourhood's main gay street and draws a mixed crowd. (www.theotherside.nl; Reguliersdwarsstraat 6; ⏰10am-midnight; 🚊1/2/5 Koningsplein)

Local Life
Weteringstraat

Off Prinsengracht, tiny Weteringstraat feels like a secret passage. Look out for local brown cafe (traditional Dutch pub), **Café de Wetering** (Map p70, D4; Weteringstraat 37; ⏰4pm-1am Mon-Thu, to 3am Fri, 3pm-3am Sat, 3pm-1am Sun; 🚊7/10 Spiegelgracht), a charmer with a cascade of greenery draped over the outside, a large fireplace and gloriously faded interior that wouldn't look out of place in a Vermeer painting. It's always packed with locals.

Lion Noir
COCKTAIL BAR

24 Map p70, D1

Lion Noir hosts a glamorous crowd, here for excellent cocktails as well as superlative dining on creative French-inspired dishes with an Asian twist. Interior artist Thijs Murré designed the eclectic, satisfyingly out-there interior of green walls, plants, birdcages and taxidermied birds; the greenery-shaded terrace is equally lovely. (www.lionnoir.nl; Reguliersdwarsstraat 28; ⏰noon-1am Mon-Thu, to 3am Fri, 6pm-3am Sat, 6pm-1am Sun; 🚊1/2/5 Koningsplein)

Van Dyck Bar
CLUB

25 Map p70, B3

Van Dyck brings Ibiza-style clubbing to Amsterdam, with a heavyweight mix of international and local DJs who know how to work the twenty-something up-for-it crowd. There's usually no cover before midnight; dress up to get past the door. (www.vandyckbar.com; Korte Leidsedwarsstraat 28-32; ⏰10pm-4am Wed, Thu & Sun, to 5am Fri & Sat; 🚊1/2/5/7/10 Leidseplein)

Club Up
CLUB

26 Map p70, B3

Garage, house, funk, soul, hip-hop, techno, live bands and performance art keep the punters happy at this small, quirky club. Entrance is occasionally through social club De Kring, at Kleine Gartmanplantsoen 7-9; check the Club Up website for details. (📞020-623 69 85; www.clubup.nl; Korte

Leliedwarsstraat 26; ⏰11pm-4am Thu, to 5am Fri & Sat; 🚊1/2/5/7/10 Leidseplein)

Eijlders
BROWN CAFE

27 Map p70, A2

During WWII, this stained-glass-trimmed brown cafe (traditional Dutch pub) was a meeting place for artists who refused to toe the cultural line imposed by the Nazis, and the spirit lingers on. It's still an artists' cafe, with waistcoated waiters and a low-key feel by day, but it gets noisier at night, fitting with its Leidseplein surrounds. (www.cafeeijlders.com; Korte Leidsedwarsstraat 47; ⏰4.30pm-1am Mon-Wed, from noon Thu, noon-2am Fri & Sat, noon-midnight Sun; 🚊1/2/5/7/10 Leidseplein)

Pata Negra
BAR

28 Map p70, G4

Ablaze with tiling the colour of sunshine, this Spanish tapas bar has an agreeably battered interior and its margaritas are the business. It gets busy with a lively crowd downing sangria with garlic-fried shrimps and grilled sardines (tapas €6 to €12.50). (www.pata-negra.nl; Utrechtsestraat 124; ⏰noon-1am Sun-Thu, to 3am Fri & Sat; 🚊4 Prinsengracht)

Taboo Bar
GAY

29 Map p70, E1

Gay favourite Taboo has plentiful two-for-one happy hours (6pm to 7pm – to 8pm on Sunday – and 1am to 2am). It's snug inside, though on warmer

days everyone spills out onto the street. On Wednesdays, cocktails cost €6 and a drag show and competitions like 'pin the tail on the sailor' take place. (www.taboobar.nl; Reguliersdwarsstraat 45; ⏰5pm-3am Mon-Thu, to 4am Fri, 4pm-4am Sat, 4pm-3am Sun; 📶; 🚊1/2/5 Koningsplein)

Escape
CLUB

30 Map p70, F1

Running since the '90s, this huge club gets busy with a happy crowd of twentysomethings, here for the cream of local and international DJs, who rock several dance floors with a soundtrack of house, electro, techno and pop. Escape regularly hosts theme nights such as House Rules and Brainwash. There's a video-screen-filled studio and an adjoining cafe. (www.escape.nl; Rembrandtplein 11; ⏰11pm-4am Thu & Sun, to 5am Fri & Sat; 🚊4/9/14 Rembrandtplein)

De Kroon BAR

31 🍴 Map p70, F1

Rembrandtplein's renovated *grand café* De Kroon dates from 1898. It has dizzyingly high ceilings, armchairs to sink into and glittering chandeliers. There's a a long list of cocktails, wine and beers, plus a barbecue-oriented menu of grilled fish and meat. It converts into a club on Friday and Saturday nights. (www.dekroon.nl; Rembrandtplein 17; ⊙4pm-1am Mon-Thu & Sun, to 3am Fri & Sat; 🚊4/9/14 Rembrandtplein)

Montmartre GAY

32 🍴 Map p70, F1

A crammed gay bar that's long been a local favourite. It's known for its Dutch music, and patrons sing (or scream) along to recordings of Dutch ballads and old top-40 hits. There's

Q Local Life
NeL

A stately white house on a hidden-away square, **NeL** (www.nelamstelveld. nl; Amstelveld 12; ⊙10am-1am Sun-Thu, to 3am Fri & Sat; 🚊4 Prinsengracht) is a contender for having the best terrace in Amsterdam. Outside, mature trees provide a canopy that dapples the sunshine on a good day – it's hard to believe it's so close to Rembrandtplein. Inside there's a mellow brasserie on one side and a stylish bar on the other.

also a lively program of karaoke, drag, and '80s and '90s hits. (www.cafemontmartre.nl; Halvemaansteeg 17; ⊙5pm-1am Sun-Thu, to 4am Fri & Sat; 🚊4/9/14 Rembrandtplein)

Whiskey Café L&B BAR

33 🍴 Map p70, B3

If amber spirits are your thing, you're in luck: this friendly, busy bar has 1350 (yes, 1350!) different varieties from Scotland, Ireland, America and Japan. The knowledgable bar staff will help you navigate the list. (Korte Leidsedwarsstraat 92; ⊙8pm-3am Mon-Thu, to 4am Fri & Sat, 5pm-3am Sun; 🚊1/2/5/7/10 Leidseplein)

Entertainment

Pathé Tuschinskitheater CINEMA

34 ⭐ Map p70, F1

This fantastical cinema, with a facade that's a prime example of the Amsterdam School of architecture, is worth visiting for its sumptuous art deco interior alone. The *grote zaal* (main auditorium) is the most stunning; it generally screens blockbusters, while the smaller theatres play arthouse and indie films. Visit the interior on an Audiotour (€10) when films aren't playing. (www.pathe.nl; Reguliersbreestraat 26-34; ⊙11.30am-12.30am; 🚊4/9/14 Rembrandtplein)

Pathé Tuschinskitheater

Melkweg
LIVE MUSIC

35 ⭐ Map p70, A2

In a former dairy, the nonprofit 'Milky Way' offers a dazzling galaxy of diverse gigs, featuring both DJs and live bands. One night it's electronica, the next reggae or punk, and the next heavy metal. Roots, rock and mellow singer-songwriters all get stage time too. Check out the website for information on its cutting-edge cinema, theatre and multimedia offerings. (Milky Way; www.melkweg.nl; Lijnbaansgracht 234a; ⊘6pm-1am; 🚊1/2/5/7/10 Leidseplein)

Paradiso
LIVE MUSIC

36 ⭐ Map p70, B3

In 1968, a beautiful old church turned into the 'Cosmic Relaxation Center Paradiso'. Today, the vibe is less hippy than funked-up odyssey, with big all-nighters, themed events and indie nights. The smaller hall hosts up-and-coming bands, but there's something special about the Main Hall, where it seems the stained-glass windows might shatter under the force of the fat beats. (📞020-622 45 21; www.paradiso.nl; Weteringschans 6; ⊘hours vary; 🚊1/2/5/7/10 Leidseplein)

Jazz Café Alto
JAZZ

37 Map p70, B3

This is an intimate, atmospheric brown cafe-style venue for serious jazz and (occasionally) blues. There are live gigs nightly: doors open at 9pm but music starts around 10pm – get here early if you want to snag a seat. (www.jazz-cafe-alto.nl; Korte Leidsedwarsstraat 115; 9pm-3am Sun-Thu, to 4am Fri & Sat; 1/2/5/7/10 Leidseplein)

Sugar Factory
LIVE MUSIC

38 Map p70, A2

With a creative vibe and many eclectic events, this is not your average club. Most nights start with music (from indie rock to techno), cinema, dance or a spoken-word performance, followed by late-night DJs and dancing. Sunday's Wicked Jazz Sounds party is a sweet one, bringing DJs, musicians, singers and actors together to improvise. (www.sugarfactory.nl; Lijnbaansgracht 238; 6pm-5am; 1/2/5/7/10 Leidseplein)

Shopping

Concerto
MUSIC

39 Map p70, G3

This rambling shop is muso heaven, with a fabulous selection of new and secondhand vinyl and CDs encompassing every imaginable genre, from rockabilly to classical and beyond. It's good value and has listening facilities, plus a sofa-strewn living-room-style cafe and regular live sessions (see the website for details). (www.concerto.amsterdam/en; Utrechtsestraat 52-60; 10am-6pm Mon, Wed & Sat, to 7pm Thu & Fri, noon-6pm Sun; 4 Prinsengracht)

Young Designers United
CLOTHING

40 Map p70, C1

This sleek boutique has a stylish array of affordable items by young designers working in the Netherlands. You might spot durable basics by Agna K, handmade leggings by Leg-Inc and geometric dresses by Fenny Faber. Accessorise with YDU's select range of jewellery and bags. (YDU; www.ydu.nl; Keizersgracht 447; 1-6pm Mon, from 10am Tue-Sat; 1/2/5 Keizersgracht)

Top Tip
Photo Op: Reguliersgracht

It's easy to focus on the raucous nightlife and forget that one of Amsterdam's most romantic canals flows through the neighbourhood. The **Reguliersgracht** Map p70, F2; (4/9/14 Rembrandtplein), aka the canal of seven bridges, is especially idyllic at night when its arched spans glow with tiny gold lights. To get the money shot, stand with your back to the Thorbeckeplein and the Herengracht flowing directly in front of you to the left and right. Lean over the bridge and look straight ahead down the Reguliersgracht. Ahhh. Now kiss your sweetie.

Eduard Kramer

MaisonNL
HOMEWARES, CLOTHING

41 Map p70, G4

This little concept store sells all sorts of beautiful things you didn't realise you needed, such as Christian Lacroix crockery and cute-as-a-button mouse toys in matchboxes by Maileg. There's a clothing rack down the back. (www.maisonnl.com; Utrechtsestraat 118; ⊘10am-6pm Tue-Sat, 1-5pm Sun; 🚊4 Prinsengracht)

Eduard Kramer
ANTIQUES

42 Map p70, C3

Specialising in antique blue-and-white Dutch tiles, this engrossing, crammed-to-the-rafters shop is chock-a-block with fascinating antiques, silver candlesticks, crystal decanters, jewellery and pocket watches. (www.antique-tileshop.nl; Prinsengracht 807; ⊘11am-6pm Mon, from 10am Tue-Sat, from 1pm Sun; 🚊7/10 Spiegelgracht)

Mobilia
HOMEWARES

43 Map p70, G3

Dutch and international design is stunningly showcased at this three-storey 'lifestyle studio', with sofas, workstations, bookshelves, lighting, cushions, rugs and much more. (www.mobilia.nl; Utrechtsestraat 62; ⊘9.30am-6pm Mon-Sat; 🚊4 Prinsengracht)

Explore

Vondelpark & the South

Vondelpark has a special place in Amsterdam's heart, a lush green egalitarian space where everyone hangs out at some point: stoners, yummy mummies, cyclists, picnickers and sunbathers. Close to the park, the wealth-laden Old South holds the Van Gogh, Stedelijk and Rijksmuseum collections. To the north, there's funky Overtoom and the De Hallen food hall and cultural complex.

PAULO AMORIM/GETTY IMAGES ©

The Sights in a Day

☼ Take a spin around beloved **Vondelpark** (p94; pictured left). Long and thin – about 1.5km long and 300m wide – it's easy to explore via a morning jaunt. Eateries in the park offer sustenance. You'll see a cross-section of freewheeling Amsterdam life hanging out here.

☀ Pay homage to the arts in the afternoon (when crowds are lighter). Fortify yourself with lunch at **l'Entrecôte et les Dames** (p99), then hit the trail around the **Museumplein** (p103). You'll likely have the stamina for just the **Van Gogh Museum** (p90) and **Rijksmuseum** (p86), but kudos if you fit in the modern **Stedelijk Museum** (p97) as well. They're all lined up in a walkable row.

☾ The streets around Overtoom and Amstelveenseweg burst with stylish eateries. For dinner go for hip Dutch tapas at **Ron Gastrobar** (p99) or chic gastronomy at **Adam** (p98). Afterwards get cultured under the stars at Vondelpark's free **Openluchttheater** (p103), or listen to classical music soar in the pristine acoustics of the **Concertgebouw** (p102).

👁 Top Sights

Rijksmuseum (p86)

Van Gogh Museum (p90)

Vondelpark (p94)

❤ Best of Amsterdam

Best Eating
Ron Gastrobar (p99)

Blue Pepper (p100)

Best Shopping
VLVT (p103)

Museum Shop at the Museumplein (p103)

Best Entertainment
Concertgebouw (p102)

OCCII (p95)

Getting There

🚋 **Tram** Trams 2 and 5 from Centraal Station stop at Museumplein and the main entrance to Vondelpark; tram 2 travels along the southern side of the park along Willemsparkweg. Trams 3 and 12 cross the 1e Constantijn Huygensstraat bridge not far from the park's main entrance, and cross Kinkerstraat near De Hallen. Tram 1 from Centraal travels along Overtoom near the park's western edge.

Top Sights
Rijksmuseum

The Rijksmuseum is a magnificent repository of art, its restaurant has a Michelin star *and* it's the only museum with a cycle lane through its centre. Beautifully presented, it includes masterpieces by homegrown geniuses, such as Rembrandt, Vermeer and Van Gogh. It was conceived to hold several national and royal collections, which occupy 1.5km of gallery space and 80 rooms.

National Museum

Map p96, E2

020-674 70 00

www.rijksmuseum.nl

Museumstraat 1

adult/child €17.50/free, audio guide €5

9am-5pm

2/5 Rijksmuseum

Rembrandt's *Night Watch* (p89)

Floor 2: Golden Age Masterpieces

The museum's top draws are in the Gallery of Honour on Floor 2. After you go through the ticket gate, head right past the audio-tour desk and go up the stairs (the ones by the sign marked 'The Collection'). Walk back to the next set of stairs and ascend – you're following the '1600–1700' signs. Eventually you'll come to the Great Hall. Push open the glass doors and behold the Golden Age's greatest works.

Frans Hals

The first room displays several paintings by Frans Hals, who painted with broad brushstrokes and a fluidity that was unique for the time. *The Merry Drinker* (1628–30) shows his style in action. No one knows who the gent with the beer glass is, but it's clear he's enjoying himself after a hard day of work.

Johannes (Jan) Vermeer

The next room holds popular Vermeer works. Check out the dreamy *Kitchen Maid* (1660) for Vermeer's famed attention to detail. See the holes in the wall? The nail with shadow? In *Woman in Blue Reading a Letter* (1663) Vermeer uses a different style. He shows only parts of objects, such as the tables and chairs, leaving the viewer to figure out the rest.

Jan Steen

Another Jan hangs across the hall from Vermeer. Jan Steen became renowned for painting chaotic households, such as the one in *The Merry Family* (1668). Everyone is having such a good time in the picture, no one notices the little boy sneaking a taste of wine.

Rijksmuseum

Floor 3: 1900–2000

CoBrA
Artists

Dutch
Designers

Floor 2: 1600–1700

The Night Watch

The Jewish
Bride

Gallery of
Honour

Kitchen Maid &
Woman in Blue
Reading a Letter

The Merry
Family

Dollhouses

The
Merry
Drinker

Delftware

Great Hall

Floor 1: 1700–1900

Battle of Waterloo

Canal House
Room

Entrances

Van Gogh
Paintings

Floor 0: 1100–1600

Asian
Pavilion

Coat & Bag
Check

Keys

Cafe

Entrance to
Exhibits

Audio Tour
Desk

Ship
Models

Ticket Desk

Rembrandt

You'll pass through a room of landscape paintings, and then come to a gallery of Rembrandt's works. *The Jewish Bride* (1665), showing a couple's intimate caress, impressed Van Gogh.

Night Watch

Rembrandt's gigantic *Night Watch* (1642) takes pride of place in the room. It shows the militia led by Frans Banning Cocq. The work is actually titled *Archers under the Command of Captain Frans Banning Cocq*. The *Night Watch* name was bestowed years later, thanks to a layer of grime that gave the impression it was evening. It's since been restored to its original colours.

Delftware

Intriguing Golden Age swag fills rooms on either side of the Gallery of Honour. Delftware was the Dutch attempt to reproduce Chinese porcelain in the late 1600s. Gallery 2.22 displays scads of the delicate blue-and-white pottery.

Dollhouses

Gallery 2.20 is devoted to mind-blowing dollhouses. Merchant's wife Petronella Oortman employed carpenters, glassblowers and silversmiths to make the 700 items inside her dollhouse, using the same materials as they would for full-scale versions.

Floor 3: 1900–2000

The uppermost floor holds a fairly limited collection. It includes avant-garde, childlike paintings by Karel Appel, Constant Nieuwenhuys and their CoBrA compadres (a post-WWII movement) and cool furnishings by Dutch designers such as Gerrit Rietveld and Michel de Klerk.

Floor 1: 1700–1900

Highlights on Floor 1 include the *Battle of Waterloo*, the Rijksmuseum's largest painting (in Gallery 1.12). Three Van Gogh paintings hang in Gallery 1.18. Gallery 1.16 recreates a gilded, 18th-century canal-house room.

Floor 0: 1100–1600

This is an awesome floor for lovers of curiosities and less-visited arts. The Special Collections present peculiar tidbits such as locks, keys, magic lanterns, old dresses, goblets and ship models. The Asia Pavilion, a separate structure that's often devoid of crowds, holds first-rate artworks from China, Indonesia, Japan, India, Thailand and Vietnam.

Facade & Gardens

Pierre Cuypers designed the 1885 building. Check out the exterior, which mixes neo-Gothic and Dutch Renaissance styles. The museum's gardens – aka the 'outdoor gallery' – host big-name sculpture exhibitions at least once per year. They're free to stroll and offer roses, hedges, fountains and a cool greenhouse year-round.

Top Sights
Van Gogh Museum

This wonderful museum holds the world's largest Van Gogh collection. It's a poignant experience to see the perma-queues outside, then trace the painter's tragic yet breathtakingly productive life. Opened in 1973 to house the collection of Vincent's younger brother, Theo, the museum comprises some 200 paintings and 500 drawings by Vincent and his contemporaries, including Gauguin and Monet.

⊙ Map p96, D3

☎ 020-570 52 00

www.vangoghmuseum.com

Museumplein 6

adult/child €17/free, audio guide €5/3

⊙ 9am-7pm Sun-Thu, to 9pm Sat mid-Jul–Aug, to 6pm Sat-Thu Sep–mid-Jul, to 5pm Jan-Mar, to 10pm Fri

🚋 2/3/5/12 Van Baerlestraat

Entrance & Set-up

In 2015 a swish extension and entrance hall added 800 sq metres of space to the museum, which now spreads over four levels, moving chronologically from Floor 0 (aka the ground floor) to Floor 3. It's still a manageable size; allow a couple of hours or so to browse the galleries.

Potato Eaters

Van Gogh's earliest works – shadowy and crude – are from his time in the Dutch countryside and in Antwerp between 1883 and 1885. He was particularly obsessed with peasants – *The Potato Eaters* (1885) is his most famous painting from this period.

Bible & Skeleton

Still Life with Bible (1885) is another early work, one which shows his religious inclination. The burnt-out candle is said to represent the recent death of his father, who was a Protestant minister. *Skeleton with Burning Cigarette* (1886) was painted when Van Gogh was a student at Antwerp's Royal Academy of Fine Arts.

Self-portraits

In 1886 Van Gogh moved to Paris, where his brother, Theo, was working as an art dealer. Vincent wanted to master the art of portraiture, but was too poor to pay for models. Several self-portraits resulted. You can see his palette begin to brighten as he comes under the influence of the Impressionists in the city.

Sunflowers

In 1888 Van Gogh left for Arles in Provence to delve into its landscapes. *Sunflowers* (1889) and other blossoms that shimmer with intense Mediterranean light are from this period.

☑ Top Tips

▶ Book ahead online (at least a few days ahead) or get a Museumkaart to skip the lengthiest museum queues in town. If you have an I Amsterdam Card, you'll still have to queue for tickets.

▶ Arrive before 11am or visit when it's late on Friday to avoid the crowds.

▶ Take time to attend the interesting workshops.

✕ Take a Break

There's a restaurant and cafe in the Van Gogh Museum, which are nothing special but they're fine if you need a breather.

The informal, bright and breezy **Seafood Bar** (☎020-670 83 55; www.theseafoodbar.nl; Van Baerlestraat 5; mains €14-37; ⏱noon-10pm; ♿; ☐2/5 Van Baerlestraat) does an excellent plateful of fish and chips, or shellfish platters served on beds of ice.

Van Gogh Museum

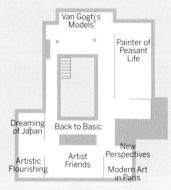

Floor 1

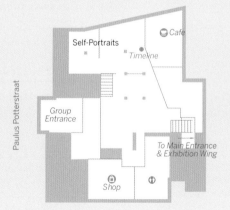

Floor 0

The Yellow House & Bedroom

Other paintings from his time in Arles include *The Yellow House* (1888), a rendering of the abode Van Gogh rented in town, intending to start an artists' colony with Gauguin. *The Bedroom* (1888) depicts Van Gogh's sleeping quarters at the house. It was in 1888 that Van Gogh sliced off part of his ear.

Wheatfield with Crows

Van Gogh had himself committed to an asylum in St Remy in 1889. While there, he painted several landscapes with cypress and olive trees, and went wild with *Irises*. In 1890 he went north to Auvers-sur-Oise. *Wheatfield with Crows* (1890), one of his last paintings, is an ominous work finished shortly before his suicide.

Extras

The museum has multiple listening stations for diverse recordings of Van Gogh's letters, mainly to and from his closest brother Theo, who championed his work. The museum has categorised all of Van Gogh's letters online at www.vangoghletters.org. There are daily workshops (for adults and kids) where, suitably inspired, you can create your own works of art.

Other Artists

Thanks to Theo van Gogh's prescient collecting and that of the museum's

Van Gogh's *Self-Portrait with Pipe and Glass* (1887)

curators, you'll also see works by Vincent's contemporaries, including Gauguin, Monet and Henri de Toulouse-Lautrec.

Exhibition Wing

The influential Dutch architect Gerrit Rietveld designed the museum's main building. Behind it, reaching towards the Museumplein, is a separate wing (opened in 1999) designed by Kisho Kurokawa and commonly referred to as 'the Mussel'. It hosts temporary exhibitions by big-name artists.

Top Sights
Vondelpark

Amsterdam's favoured playground is the green lozenge-shaped expanse of Vondelpark, with its 47 hectares of lawns, ponds and winding paths receiving 12 million visitors a year. All of Amsterdam life is here: visitors, rollerskaters, yummy mummies, kids and stoners. There's a constantly whizzing parade of bikes and on a sunny day you can hardly move for picnics all around the grass.

👁 Map p96, E2

www.hetvondelpark.net

🚋 2 Amstelveenseweg

Joost van den Vondel monument

Vondel Statue

The English-style gardens, with ponds, lawns, footbridges and winding footpaths, were laid out in 1865 and originally known as Nieuwe Park (New Park). In 1867 sculptor Louis Royer added a statue of famed poet and playwright Joost van den Vondel (1587–1679). Amsterdammers began referring to the place as Vondel's Park, which led to it being renamed.

Hippy Remnants

During the late 1960s and early 1970s, Dutch authorities turned the park into a temporary open-air dormitory for the droves of hippies who descended on Amsterdam. The sleeping bags are long gone, but remnants of the era live on in the squats that fringe the park, such as **OT301** (www.ot301.nl; Overtoom 301; ⬚1 Jan Pieter Heijestraat) and **OCCII** (☏020-671 77 78; www.occii.org; Amstelveenseweg 134; ⏰hours vary; ♿; ⬚2 Amstelveenseweg), now both legalised into underground cultural centres.

Gardens & Grounds

The park's 47 hectares encourage visitors to get out and explore. The rose garden, with some 70 different species, was added in 1936. It's in the middle of the park; signs point the way. Neon-green parrots flit through the trees; the former pets were released into the wild decades ago. The park also shelters several cafes, playgrounds and a wonderful outdoor theatre.

Picasso Sculpture

Art is strewn throughout the park, with 69 sculptures dotted throughout the leafy environs. Among them is Picasso's soaring abstract work *Figure découpée l'Oiseau* (*The Bird*), better known locally as *The Fish* (1965), which he donated for the park's centenary.

☑ Top Tips

▶ It's great to glide around and explore the park by bike. Arrive here by bike or hire one nearby.

▶ Sunday is funday at Vondelpark, when there's almost a festival atmosphere on sunny days.

▶ Look out for events at the park's outdoor Openluchttheater (p103) during summer.

✗ Take a Break

The elegant cake-stand architecture of **'t Blauwe Theehuis** (www.blauwe theehuis.nl; Vondelpark 5; ⏰9am-10pm; 📶; ⬚2 Jacob Obrechtstraat) makes for a lovely spot for food and drinks in the park.

200 m
0.1 miles

E

Prinsengr

Boerenwetering

Hobbemakade

Leidsestr

Marnixstr

Max
Euweplein

Weteringschans

Singelgracht

Hobbemastr

Roelof Hartpl

Nassaukade

D

Jacob van
Lennepkade

Bosboom
Toussaintstr

1e Helmersstr

3e Helmersstr

2e Helmersstr

Vondelstr

Stadhouderskade

Rijksmuseum 🅾

Diamond
Museum 3 🅾

Van Baerlestr

Jan Willem
Brouwersstr

Roelof Hartstr

Gerard Terborg 🗙10

E

Vossiusstr Hooftstr

Pieter Cornelisz Hooftstr

Jan Luijkenstr

House of Bols 🅾4

Paulus Potterstr

Stedelijk Museum 🅾1

**Van Gogh
Museum**

Museum-
plein 🅾

Johannes
Vermeerstr

Horthorststr

Museum 🅾

Nicolaas Maesstr

Frans van Mierisstr

Ruysdaelstr

🗙9

17🅾

OUD ZUID

Concertgebouwplein

Banstr

Vondelpark 🅾

C

Bilderdijkstr

1e Constantijn Huygenstr

2e Constantijn Huygenstr

🅿19

2 🅾 Hollandsche
Manege

14 🗙

OUD WEST

Jacob van Lennepkanaal

Overtoom

Vondelstr

18 🅾

Van Eeghenstr

Willemsparkweg

Cornelis Schuytstr

Koninginneweg

20🗙

Valeriusstr

Johannes Verhulststr

De Lairessestr

Reijnier Vinkeleskade

Noorder Amstel Kar

B

13🅾

Wilhelminastr

Jan Pieter Heijestr

16🗙

Gerard
Brandtstr

1e Helmersstr

🗙7

Vondelpark

Koningslaan

A

🗙5

🗙11

🗙6

Amstelveenseweg

15🗙

For reviews see	
🅾 Top Sights	p86
🅾 Sights	p97
🗙 Eating	p98
🅾 Drinking	p101
🅾 Entertainment	p102
🅾 Shopping	p103

MERTEN SNIJDERS/GETTY IMAGES ©

Stedelijk Museum

Sights

Stedelijk Museum
MUSEUM

1 ⊙ Map p96, D3

This fabulous museum houses the collection amassed by postwar curator Willem Sandberg. Displays rotate but you'll see an amazing selection featuring works by Picasso, Matisse, Mondrian, Van Gogh, Rothko, De Kooning, Warhol and more, plus an exhuberant De Appel mural and great temporary exhibitions. The building was originally a bank, built in 1895 to a neo-Renaissance design by AM Weissman, and the modern extension is nicknamed 'the bathtub' for reasons that will be obvious when you see it. (☏020-573 29 11; www.stedelijk.nl; Museumplein 10; adult/child €17.50/free; ☺10am-6pm Sat-Thu, to 10pm Fri; ☐2/3/5/12 Van Baerlestraat)

Hollandsche Manege
HORSE RIDING

2 ⊙ Map p96, C2

The neoclassical Hollandsche Manege is a surprise to discover just outside Vondelpark. Entering is like stepping back in time, into a grandiose indoor riding school inspired by the famous Spanish Riding School in Vienna. Designed by AL van Gendt and built in 1882, it retains its charming horse-head facade and has a large riding arena and interior. (📞020-618 09 42; www.dehollandschemanege.nl; Vondelstraat 140; adult/child €8/4, private riding lessons per 30/60min €38/62; ⏱10am-5pm; 🚊1 1e Constantijn Huygensstraat)

Diamond Museum
MUSEUM

 3 ◎ Map p96, E2

The extensive bling on display at the small, low-tech Diamond Museum is all clever re-creations. You get a lot of background on the history of the trade and various historic sparkly crowns and jewels. Here you'll learn how Amsterdam was the globe's diamond

Local Life
De Hallen Cultural Centre

Built in 1902, these red-brick tram sheds were then used as a squat before being turned into this breathtaking sky-lit space in 2014. The cultural complex now incorporates a food hall, **Foodhallen** (Map p96, C1; www.foodhallen.nl; De Hallen, Hannie Dankbaar Passage 3; dishes €3-20; ⏱11am-11.30pm Sun-Thu, to 1am Fri & Sat; 👶; 🚊17 Ten Katestraat), family-friendly brasserie, library, Dutch design shops, a bike seller/repairer, a cinema and a hotel. Regular events held inside include themed weekend markets (www.localgoodsmarkets.nl) such as organic produce or Dutch design). A lively daily (except Sunday) street market, Ten Katemarkt, takes place outside.

trade epicentre for many centuries, where local Jews dominated the cutting and polishing business, and how the business moved to Antwerp after WWII following the decimation of the Jewish population here. (www.diamantmuseumamsterdam.nl; Paulus Potterstraat 8; adult/child €10/free; ⏱9am-5pm; 🚊2/5 Hobbemastraat)

House of Bols
MUSEUM

4 ◎ Map p96, D3

Cheesy but fun: here you undertake an hour's self-guided tour through this *jenever* (Dutch gin) museum. In the 'Hall of Taste' you'll try to differentiate different scents and flavours, while in the 'Distillery Room' you'll learn about the process of extraction. You'll learn more about the history of gin than you would think possible, and get to try shaking your own cocktail, plus drink a Bols confection of your choice at the end. (www.houseofbols.com; Paulus Potterstraat 14; admission incl 1 cocktail €16.50, over 18yr only; ⏱1-6.30pm Sun-Thu, to 9pm Fri & Sat; 🚊2/5 Hobbemastraat)

Eating

Adam
GASTRONOMY €€

 5 ✗ Map p96, A3

This seriously gourmet, chic and intimate restaurant serves exquisitely presented fare, such as veal cheek with lentils and bay sauce and *côte de bœuf* (on-the-bone rib steak) for two. Dessert is either a cheese platter or a chef's surprise. Paired wines are available for €7.50 per glass. (📞020-233 98 52; www.restaurantadam.nl; Overtoom 515; mains €21-23, 3-/4-/5-/6-course menus €37.50/45/52.50/60; ⏱6-10.30pm Tue-Sat; 🚊1 Overtoomsesluis)

Braai BBQ Bar
BARBECUE €

6 🍴 Map p96, A3

Once a *haringhuis* (herring stand), this tiny place is now a street-food-style barbecue bar, with a great canalside setting. Braai's speciality is marinated, barbecued ribs (half or full rack) and roasted sausages, but there are veggie options too. Cards are preferred, but it accepts cash. Tables scatter under the trees alongside the water. (www.braaiamsterdam.nl; Schinkel-havenkade 1; dishes €6-12; ⏱4-9.30pm; 🚊1 Overtoomsesluis)

Dikke Graaf
MEDITERRANEAN €€

7 🍴 Map p96, B2

This local favourite features industrial-styled copper lamps and scrubbed-wood tables, and opens to an olive-tree-ringed terrace. It's a truly fabulous spot for *borrel* (drinks), with gin cocktails, by-the-glass wines and bar snacks like oysters, bruschetta, charcuterie and Manchego sheep's cheese, and/or heartier, nightly changing meat, fish and pasta dishes. (📞020-223 77 56; www.dikkegraaf.nl; Wilhelminastraat 153; mains €13-25; ⏱kitchen 3-10pm Wed-Sun; 🚊1 Rhijnvis Feithstraat)

Ron Gastrobar
DUTCH €€

8 🍴 Map p96, A4

Ron Blaauw ran his two-Michelin-star restaurant in these pared-down, spacious designer premises before turning it into a more affordable 'gastrobar' (still Michelin-starred), whereby you get the quality without the formality or the need to settle down for five courses. He serves around 25 gourmet tapas-style dishes, marrying surprising flavours such as foie gras, raspberry and yoghurt. (📞020-496 19 43; www.rongastrobar.nl; Sophialaan 55; dishes €15; ⏱noon-2.30pm & 5.30-10.30pm; 📶; 🚊2 Amstelveenseweg)

l'Entrecôte et les Dames
FRENCH €€

9 🍴 Map p96, D3

With a double-height wall made from wooden drawers and a wrought-iron balcony, this restaurant has a simple menu of steak or fish: go for the *entrecôte* (premium beef steak), and save room for scrumptious desserts: perhaps chocolate mousse, *tarte au citron* (lemon tart) or *crêpes au Grand Marnier*. (📞020-679 88 88; www.entrecote-et-les-dames.nl; Van Baerlestraat 47-49; lunch mains €13.50, 2-course dinner menu €24.50; ⏱noon-3pm & 5.30-10pm; 🚊16/24 Museumplein)

Local Life
Vondelpark Squats

Fringing Vondelpark are several squats that have gone legit and been turned into alternative cultural centres.

Graffiti-covered ex-squat OT301 (p95) hosts an eclectic line-up of bands and DJs. There are two bars and restaurant, **De Peper** (Map p96, B3; ☎020-412 29 54; www.depeper. org; Overtoom 301; mains €7-10; ⊙6-8.30pm, bar to 1am Tue, Thu, Fri & Sun; ✈; ☒1 Jan Pieter Heijestraat), serving cheap, organic, vegan meals.

Underground, mostly local bands play at ex-squat OCCII (p95), which also has a collectively run, no-frills vegan restaurant, **Eetcafé MKZ** (Map p96, A4; ☎020-679 07 12; www.veganamsterdam.org/mkz; 1e Schinkelstraat 16; mains from €5; ⊙from 7pm Tue & Thu-Sat; ✈; ☒2 Amstelveenseweg).

La Falote DUTCH €€

10 Map p96, E4

Snug little La Falote, with its chequered tablecloths, focuses on daily changing Dutch home-style dishes, such as calf liver, meatballs with endives, or stewed fish with beets and mustard sauce. The prices are a bargain in an otherwise ritzy neighbourhood; and wait till the owner brings out the accordion. (☎020-662 54 54; www.lafalote.nl; Roelof Hartstraat 26; mains €15-25; ⊙1.30-9pm Mon-Sat; ☒3/5/12/24 Roelof Hartplein)

Moer INTERNATIONAL €€€

11 Map p96, A3

Attached to the Tire Station hotel, Moer has a plate-glass wall onto the street, artful moss and green credentials – the ceiling is insulated by plants and heating is channelled from the kitchen. Chefs Dirk Mooren and Cas van de Pol cook up a storm in the open kitchen, serving largely organic and sustainable food with lots of vegetarian choices. (☎020-820 33 30; Amstelveenseweg 7; dishes €9-20; ⊙noon-10pm; ✈; ☒Overtoom)

Blue Pepper INDONESIAN €€€

12 Map p96, D1

This is one of Amsterdam's finest gourmet Indonesian restaurants, where Chef Sonja Pereira serves beautifully presented work-of-art Indonesian cuisine in an intimate white-walled dining room. The rijsttafel (Indonesian banquet) includes specialities from across the islands, such as wild scallops with saffron, orange, sea greens and macadamia nuts, or venison with sambal goreng of laos, ginger and sweet pepper. (☎020-489 70 39; www.restaurantbluepepper.com; Nassaukade 366; rijsttafel per person €57-65; ⊙6-10pm; ✈; ☒7/10 Raamplein)

BORIS B/SHUTTERSTOCK ©

BELCAMPO

De Hallen Cultural Centre (p98)

Drinking

Edel
BAR

13 🚇 Map p96, B1

Edel on Het Sieraad's waterfront has lots of waterside seating as it's at the sweet spot where two canals cross. Inside and out it's full of creative types who work in the local buildings. With hipster staff and creative food on offer, its blonde-wood interior comes into its own in summer, lit by a canopy of twinkling fairy lights after dark. (www.edelamsterdam.nl; Postjesweg 1; ☺10am-1am Sun-Thu, to 3am Fri & Sat; 🚊7/17 Kinkerstraat)

Lot Sixty One
COFFEE

14 🚇 Map p96, C1

Look downstairs to the open cellar to see (and better still, smell) fresh coffee beans being roasted at this street-wise spot. Beans are sourced from individual ecofriendly farms; varieties include chocolate-orange Fivr from Brazil, citrussy Kii from Kenya and toffee stonefruit Bombora. All coffees are double shots (unless you specify otherwise); watch Kinkerstraat's passing parade from benches at the front. (www.lotsixtyonecoffee.com; Kinkerstraat 112; ☺8am-5pm Mon-Fri, 9am-5pm Sat, 10am-5pm Sun; 🚊3/12 Bilderdijkstraat)

Café Bédier

BROWN CAFE

15 🚇 Map p96, A4

Café Bédier is a post-work favourite with a terrace out the front that's often so crowded on a sunny evening that it looks like a street party in full swing. Inside it also gets rammed; the leather-upholstered wall panels, modular seats and hardwood floors put a 21st-century twist on classic brown cafe decor. Top-notch bar food, too. (📞020-662 44 15; Sophialaan 36; ⏰noon-1am Mon-Thu, to 3am Fri, 11am-3am Sat, to 1am Sun; 🚋2 Amstelveenseweg)

Golden Brown Bar

BAR

16 🚇 Map p96, B2

This perennially hip, two-level bar with painted brickwork and cool colour palette attracts a young professional crowd that spills out onto the pavement. In winter, the cream-and-brown interior with its mod woodwork and neon-pink-lit bar offers a stylish respite from the chill, especially if you snag a seat on the faux-velvet couch. (www.goldenbrownbar.nl; Jan Pieter Heijestraat 146; ⏰11am-1am Mon-Thu, to 3am Fri & Sat; 📞; 🚋1 Jan Pieter Heijestraat)

Entertainment

Concertgebouw

CLASSICAL MUSIC

17 ⭐ Map p96, D3

The Concert Hall was built in 1888 by AL van Gendt, who managed to engineer its near-perfect acoustics. Bernard Haitink, former conductor of the Royal Concertgebouw Orchestra, remarked that the world-famous hall was the orchestra's best instru-

---

Understand
The Golden Age

The Golden Age spans roughly the 17th century, when Holland was at the peak of its powers. It's the era when Rembrandt painted, when city planners built the canals and when Dutch ships conquered the seas.

It started when trading rival Antwerp was retaken by the Spaniards in the late 16th century, and merchants, skippers and artisans flocked to Amsterdam. A new moneyed society emerged. Persecuted Jews from Portugal and Spain also fled to Amsterdam. Not only did they introduce the diamond industry, they also knew of trade routes to the West and East Indies.

Enter the Dutch East India Company, which wrested the Asian spice trade from the Portuguese. It soon grew into the world's richest corporation, with more than 50,000 employees and a private army. Its sister, the Dutch West India Company, traded with Africa and the Americas and was at the centre of the American slave trade. In 1672 Louis XIV of France invaded the Low Countries, and the era known as the Dutch Golden Age ended.

ment. Free half-hour concerts take place Wednesdays at 12.30pm from September to June; arrive early. Try the Last Minute Ticket Shop (www.lastminuteticketshop.nl) for half-price seats to all other performances. (Concert Hall; 📞020-671 83 45; www.concertgebouw.nl; Concertgebouwplein 10; 🕐box office 1-7pm Mon-Fri, to 7pm Sat & Sun; 🚊3/5/12/16/24 Museumplein)

Openluchttheater
THEATRE

18 ⭐ Map p96, C3

Vondelpark's marvellous open-air theatre hosts free concerts in summer, with a laid-back, festival feel, as you might expect from Amsterdam's hippiest park. The program includes world music, dance, theatre and more. You can make a reservation (€5 per seat) on the website up to 1½ hours prior to showtime. (Open-Air Theatre; www.openluchttheater.nl; Vondelpark 5a; 🕐May–mid-Sep; ; 🚊1 1e Constantijn Huygensstraat)

Shopping

Pied à Terre
BOOKS

19 🔒 Map p96, C2

Travel lovers will be in heaven in the galleried, sky-lit interior of Europe's largest travel bookshop. If it's travel or outdoor-related, you can dream over it here: gorgeous globes, travel guides in multiple languages (especially English) and over 600,000 maps. Order a coffee and plan your next trip. (📞020-627 44 55; www.piedaterre.nl;

Top Tip

Museumplein

Amsterdam's most famous museums cluster around this **public square** (🚊2/3/5/12 Van Baerlestraat), which has a skateboard ramp, playground, winter ice-skating rink and 2m-high *I Amsterdam* sculpture (a favourite climbing structure/photo op). It's a popular picnic spot; there are food and craft stalls on the third Sunday of the month. The space is also used for public concerts and events. At the **Museum Shop at the Museumplein** (Map p96, E3; Hobbemastraat; 🕐shop 10am-6pm, ticket window for museum entrance 8.30am-6pm; 🚊2/5 Hobbemastraat) you can pick up posters, cards and other art souvenirs from both institutions (and avoid the museums' entrance queues).

Overtoom 135-137; 🕐1-6pm Mon, 10am-6pm Tue, Wed & Fri, to 9pm Thu, to 5pm Sat; 🚊1 1e Constantijn Huygensstraat)

VLVT
FASHION & ACCESSORIES

20 🔒 Map p96, C4

Up-and-coming Dutch-designed fashion for women is stocked at this chic, light-filled boutique, featuring Dutch and international designers, all carefully curated and including labels such as Elisabetta Franchi, Pinko, Pierre Balmain and Furla of Zoe Karssen. (www.vlvt.nl; Cornelis Schuytstraat 22; 🕐noon-6pm Mon, 10am-6pm Tue-Sat, noon-5pm Sun; 🚊2 Cornelis Schuytstraat)

Explore

De Pijp

A hotbed of creativity, village-like De Pijp is home to a diverse mix of labourers, immigrants, intellectuals, prostitutes and young urban-ites. Marvel at the scene at Amsterdam's largest street market, the colourful Albert Cuypmarkt (pictured above), and the outstanding eateries and free-spirited *cafés* (pubs) that surround it.

The Sights in a Day

☀️ Brunch is a big to-do in De Pijp, so start off with a bountiful morning feed at **Bakers & Roasters** (p110) or an all-avocado feast at **Avocado Show** (p110). Then browse the cool shops. **Hutspot** (p114) features Dutch design decor. Fashion buffs can check out the wares at **Good Genes** (p115).

🌞 For lunch grab a burger at the **Butcher** (p111). Not hungry after the big breakfast? Opt for a coffee pick-me-up at **Scandinavian Embassy** (p111). Then prepare for the **Heineken Experience** (p109), the multimedia brewery tour where you'll get shaken up, bottled and 'become' a beer. If you go in the late afternoon, the tasting at the end provides a built-in happy hour.

🌙 You're spoiled for choice come dinnertime. There's **Volt** (p112) for Mediterranean bites under twinkling lights or **Graham's Kitchen** (p112) for cutting-edge gastronomy. In the evening, catch a film at **Rialto Cinema** (p114) or settle in for house-brewed beer at **Brouwerij Troost** (p113) or organic wine at **Glouglou** (p114).

For a local's day in De Pijp, see p106.

🔍 **Local Life**

Discovering Bohemian De Pijp (p106)

 Best of Amsterdam

Best Eating

Avocado Show (p110)

Butcher (p111)

Graham's Kitchen (p112)

Bakers & Roasters (p110)

Scandinavian Embassy (p111)

Best Parks & Gardens

Sarphatipark (p107)

Getting There

🚊 **Tram** Trams 16 and 24 roll north–south from Centraal Station along Ferdinand Bolstraat right by De Pijp's main sights. Tram 4 travels from Rembrandtplein, while tram 3 cuts east–west across the neighbourhood. Tram 12 cuts through De Pijp en route to Vondelpark. (Beware of old transport maps; tram 25 no longer runs.)

Ⓜ **Metro** From mid-2018, the Noord/Zuidlijn (north–south metro line) will serve De Pijp, with entrances at the corner of Ferdinand Bolstraat and Albert Cuypstraat, and at the corner of Ferdinand Bolstraat and Ceintuurbaan.

Local Life
Discovering Bohemian De Pijp

Artists and intellectuals have hung out in De Pijp since the 19th century, when the former slum's cheap housing drew them in. The district still wafts bohemian flair, from the spicy market at its epicentre to the cool-cat cafes and retro shops that jam its streets. A surprise red-light area also makes an appearance.

① Albert Cuypmarkt

The half-mile-long **Albert Cuypmarkt** (http://albertcuyp-markt.amsterdam; Albert Cuypstraat, btwn Ferdinand Bolstraat & Van Woustraat; ⊗9.30am-5pm Mon-Sat; 🚊16/24 Albert Cuypstraat) is Amsterdam's largest and busiest market. Vendors from Indonesia, Suriname, Morocco and other countries loudly tout their gadgets, clothing and spices, while Dutch snack stalls tempt with herring sandwiches and caramel-syrup-filled

stroopwafels. Graze as you gaze at the whirl of goods on offer.

❷ Katsu

Relaxed **Katsu** (www.katsu.nl; 1e Van der Helststraat 70; ⏱10am-midnight Mon-Thu, to 1am Fri & Sat, 11am-midnight Sun; 🚋16/24 Albert Cuypstraat), De Pijp's favourite coffeeshop, brims with colourful characters. The front table with newspapers lends a bookish vibe. When seating on the ground floor and terrace gets tight, head up to the 1st-floor lounge.

❸ Sarphatipark

While Vondelpark is bigger in size and reputation, **Sarphatipark** (🚋3 2e Van der Helststraat) delivers an equally potent shot of pastoral relaxation, without the crowds. In the centre you'll see a bombastic temple with a fountain, gargoyles and a bust of Samuel Sarphati (1813–66), a Jewish doctor, businessman and urban innovator who helped define the neighbourhood.

❹ CT Coffee & Coconuts

CT Coffee & Coconuts (http://coffeeand coconuts.com; Ceintuurbaan 282-284; mains €8.50-22.50; ⏱8am-11pm; 🛜; 🚋3 Ceintuurbaan) spreads through a cathedral-like building that was a 1920s cinema. Locals flock here for brunch dishes such as coconut, almond and buckwheat pancakes and French-toast brioche with apricots. The lunch and dinner menu spans prawn tacos and tempeh burgers.

❺ Red-light Area

What the...? You're walking along Ruysdaelkade and suddenly there's a strip of **red-light windows** between 1e Jan Steenstraat and Albert Cuypstraat. It's a good place to glimpse the world's oldest profession, minus the stag parties and drunken crowds that prowl the main Red Light District in the city centre.

❻ Café Binnen Buiten

The minute there's a sliver of sunshine, **Café Binnen Buiten** (www.cafebin nenbuiten.nl; Ruysdaelkade 115; ⏱10am-1am Sun-Thu, to 3am Fri & Sat; 🚋16/24 Ruysdaelstraat) gets packed. Sure, the food's good and the bar is candlelit and cosy. But what really brings the crowds is simply the best canalside terrace in De Pijp, offering a terrific way to while away an afternoon.

❼ Record Mania

Fantastically old school, **Record Mania** (www.recordmania.nl; Ferdinand Bolstraat 30; ⏱noon-6pm Mon-Sat; 🚋16/24 Stadhouderskade) is where neighbourhood folks go for their vinyl and CDs. The shop, with old posters, stained-glass windows, and records and CDs embedded in the floor, is a treasure in itself.

❽ Barça

One of the hottest bars in De Pijp, **Barça** (www.barca.nl; Marie Heinekenplein 30-31; ⏱11am-midnight Sun-Thu, to 2am Fri & Sat; 🚋16/24 Stadhouderskade) – themed like 'Barcelona in Amsterdam' – is the heartbeat of Marie Heinekenplein. Hang out in the plush gold and dark-timber interior, or spread out onto the terrace, glass of sparkling wine in hand.

200 m
0.1 miles

Amsteldijk

Amstel

Weesperzijde

1e Oosterparkstr

Ruyschstr

Amsteldijk

Van Woustr

Sint Willibrordusstr

Rustenburgerstr

Van Ostadestr

Tolstr

Hemonystr

2e Jan Steenstr

2e van der Heijdenstr

Ceintuurbaan

Van Woustr

Hemonylaan

Govert Flinckstr

Sarphatikade

Singelgracht

De Dageraad

Telegenstr

Pieter Lodewijk Takstr

Burgemeester

Lutmastr

Jozef Israëlskade

Amstelkanaal

DE PIJP

Van der Karel du Jardinstr

2e Van der Helststr

Van Ostadestr

Rustenburgerstr

Helstplein

Sarphatipark

1e Sweelinckstr

Sarphatipark

Sarphatipark

Nicolaas Witsenkade

Stadhouderskade

2e Jacob van Campenstr

Gerard Doustr

Albert Cuypstr

Gerard Douplein

1e Van der Helststr

Sarphatipark

1e Van der Helststr

Heineken Experience

Marie Heinekenplein

Ferdinand Bolstr

1e Jan van der Heijdenstr

1e Jan Steenstr

Govert Flinckstr

Van Ostadestr

Rustenburgerstr

Cornelis Troostsstr

Jozef Israëlskade

1e Jacob van Campenstr

Quellijnstr

Daniel Stalpertstr

Frans Halsstr

Ruysdaelkade

Ruysdaelkade

Hobbemakade

Boerenwetering

ANTON_IVANOV/SHUTTERSTOCK ©

Heineken Experience

Sights

Heineken Experience BREWERY

 1 Map p108, B1

On the site of the company's old brewery, Heineken's self-guided 'Experience' provides an entertaining overview of the brewing process, with a multimedia exhibit where you 'become' a beer by getting shaken up, sprayed with water and subjected to heat. Prebooking tickets online saves adults €2 and, crucially, allows you to skip the ticket queues. Guided 2½-hour VIP tours end with a five-beer tasting and cheese pairing. Great-value Rock the City tickets include a 45-minute canal cruise to A'DAM Tower. (☏020-523 92 22; https://tickets.heinekenexperience.com; Stadhouderskade 78; adult/child self-guided tour €18/12.50, VIP guided tour €49, Rock the City ticket €25; ⏱10.30am-7.30pm Mon-Thu, to 9pm Fri-Sun; ☐16/24 Stadhouderskade)

De Dageraad ARCHITECTURE

2 Map p108, C4

Following the key *Housing Act* of 1901, which forced the city to rethink neighbourhood planning, De Dageraad housing estate was developed between 1918 and 1923 for poor families.An architect of the expressionist Amsterdam School, Piet Kramer, drew up plans for this idiosyncratic complex in collaboration with Michel de Klerk. (Dawn Housing Project; Pieter Lodewijk Takstraat; ☐4 Amstelkade)

> **Understand**
>
> ## Amsterdam School Architecture
>
> When Amsterdam School architecture started around WWI, it was as much a political movement as an aesthetic one. Architects such as Pieter Kramer and Michel de Klerk were reacting to the lavish, decadent style of neo-Renaissance buildings like Centraal Station, but also to appalling housing conditions for the poor. Their fantastical public-funded housing projects resemble shells, waves and other organic forms; they were obsessive about details, designing everything down to the house numbers. Some details were a bit paternalistic and controlling – windows high in the wall were meant to deter leaning out and gossiping with neighbours – but in general the buildings were vast improvements. The best examples to see are De Dageraad (p109) in De Pijp and Museum Het Schip (p65) near Westerpark.

Eating

Avocado Show   CAFE €

3 ⊗ Map p108, A2

A world first, this cafe uses avocado in *every* dish, often in ingeniously functional ways (burgers with avocado halves instead of buns, salad 'bowls' made from avocado slices...). Finish with avocado ice cream or sorbet. Avocado cocktails include a spicy Guaco Mary and an avocado daiquiri. It doesn't take reservations, so prepare to queue. Cards only; no cash. (www.theavocadoshow.com; Daniël Stalpertstraat 61; mains €8-15; ⊙8.30am-5pm Thu-Tue, 11am-5pm Wed; 🛜🚲; 🚊16/24 Marie Heinekenplein)

Bakers & Roasters   CAFE €

4 ⊗ Map p108, A1

Sumptuous brunch dishes served up at Brazilian/Kiwi-owned Bakers & Roasters include banana nutbread French toast with homemade banana marmalade and crispy bacon; Navajo eggs with pulled pork, avocado, mango salsa and chipotle cream; and a smoked-salmon stack with poached eggs, potato cakes and hollandaise. Wash your choice down with a fiery Bloody Mary. Fantastic pies, cakes and slices, too. (www.bakersandroasters.com; 1e Jacob van Campenstraat 54; dishes €7.50-15.50; ⊙8.30am-4pm; 🚊16/24 Stadhouderskade)

Sugo   PIZZA €

5 ⊗ Map p108, B3

Spectacular pizza slices at this two-storey restaurant are cooked daily, displayed beneath glass and warmed in ovens. Topping combinations include caramelised onion, mascarpone, walnut and black olive or potato, mushroom and truffle cream sauce. Veggies are locally sourced, while meats and cheeses are from small farms in Italy. Takeaway packaging is made from recycled paper and energy is 100% sustainable. (www.sugopizza.nl; Ferdinand Bolstraat 107; pizza €2.80-4.20; ⊙11am-10pm; 🖉; 🚋3/12 Ferdinand Bolstraat)

Sir Hummus MIDDLE EASTERN €

6 Map p108, B3

Sir Hummus is the brainchild of three young Israelis whose passion for the chickpea dip led to a London street-market stall and then this hummus-dedicated cafe. Creamy all-natural, preservative- and additive-free hummus is served with pillowy pita bread and salad; SH also makes fantastic falafels. You can eat in or take away, but arrive early before it sells out. (www.sirhummus.nl; Van der Helstplein 2; dishes €6.50-12; ⊙noon-8pm Tue-Fri, noon-5pm Sat & Sun; 🖉; 🚋3 2e Van der Helststraat)

Scandinavian Embassy CAFE €

7 Map p108, B3

Oatmeal porridge with blueberries, honey and coconut, served with goat's-milk yoghurt; salt-cured salmon on Danish rye with sheep's-milk yoghurt; muesli with strawberries; and freshly baked pastries (including cinnamon buns) make this blond-wood-panelled spot a perfect place to start the day – as does its phenomenal coffee, sourced from Scandinavian microroasteries (including a refreshing cold brew with tonic water). (http://scandinavianembassy.nl; Sarphatipark 34; dishes €4.50-11.50; ⊙7.30am-6pm Mon-Fri, 9am-6pm Sat & Sun; 🚋3 2e Van der Helststraat)

Butcher BURGERS €

8 Map p108, B2

Burgers at this sizzling spot are cooked right in front of you (behind a glass screen, so you won't get splattered). Mouthwatering choices include 'Silence of the Lamb' (with spices and tahini), the 'Codfather' (beer-battered blue cod and homemade tartar sauce), an Angus-beef truffle burger and a veggie version. Ask about its 'secret kitchen' cocktail bar. (☎020-470 78 75; http://the-butcher.com; Albert Cuypstraat 129; burgers €7.50-11.50; ⊙11am-midnight; 🚋16/24 Albert Cuypstraat)

Miss Korea BBQ KOREAN, BARBECUE €€

9 Map p108, A2

Tables at this wildly popular all-you-can-eat restaurant have inset barbecue plates to sizzle up pork belly, seasoned beef, squid, prawns and vegetables

---

Local Life
Seafood Snacks

Locals love to hit up De Pijp's herring stands on and around Albert Cuypmarkt for herring served chopped with diced onion on a fluffy bread roll. **Volendammer Vishandel** (Map p108, B2; 1e Van der Helststraat; dishes €2-5.50; ⊙8am-5pm Mon-Sat; 🚋16/24 Albert Cuypstraat) is a favourite. Dutch flags fly from this traditional *haringhuis* ('herring house', ie takeaway fish shop), which has its own fishing fleet at the seaside resort of Volendam.

yourself. You can order an unlimited number of ingredients; there's a penalty for uneaten food to minimise wastage. Korean spirits, rice wine and beers dominate the drinks menu; ice-cream flavours include green tea and black sesame. (📞020-679 06 06; www.misskorea.nl; Albert Cuypstraat 66-70; adult/child €28.50/12.50; ⏰5-11pm Tue-Sun; 🚻; 🚋16/24 Albert Cuypstraat)

Dèsa
 INDONESIAN €€

10 🍴 Map p108, B3

Named for the Indonesian word for 'village' (apt for this city, but especially this 'hood), Dèsa is wildly popular for its rijsttafel (Indonesian banquet). À la carte options include *serundeng* (spiced fried coconut), *ayam besengek* (chicken cooked in saffron and coconut milk), *sambal goreng telor* (stewed eggs in spicy Balinese sauce), and *pisang goreng* (fried banana) for dessert. (📞020-671 09 79; www.restaurantdesa.com; Ceintuurbaan 103; mains €12.50-22,

 Local Life

Café Sarphaat

Grab an outdoor table along Sarphatipark at **Café Sarphaat** (Map p108, C2; 📞020-675 15 65; Ceintuurbaan 157; ⏰9am-1am Sun-Thu, to 3am Fri & Sat; 🚋3/4 Van Woustraat), order a frothy beer and see if you don't feel like a local. This is one of the neighbourhood's most genial spots, with a lovely old bar that makes sipping a *jenever* (Dutch gin) in broad daylight seem like a good idea. Free live jazz plays most Sunday afternoons.

rijsttafel €18.50-35; ⏰5-10.30pm; 🅿; 🚋3 Ferdinand Bolstraat)

Volt
MEDITERRANEAN €€

11 🍴 Map p108, B3

Strung with coloured light bulbs, Volt is a neighbourhood gem for light tapas-style bites (olives and marinated sardines; aioli and tapenade) and more substantial mains (artichoke ravioli with walnuts and rocket (arugula); oxtail with celeriac and potato mousseline; or steak tartare with pickled beetroot). Its bar stays open until late, or head across the street to its brown *café* (pub) sibling, Gambrinus (p114). (📞020-471 55 44; www.restaurantvolt.nl; Ferdinand Bolstraat 178; mains €9-19, tapas €5-12; ⏰4-10pm Mon-Fri, 11am-10pm Sat & Sun; 🚋12 Cornelis Troostplein)

Graham's Kitchen
GASTRONOMY €€€

12 🍴 Map p108, D1

A veteran of Michelin-starred kitchens, chef Graham Mee now crafts intricate dishes at his own premises. Multicourse evening menus (no à la carte) might include a venison and crispy smoked-beetroot *macaron*, cucumber and gin-cured salmon, veal with wasabi and ghost crab, and deconstructed summer-berry crumble with wood-calamint ice cream. Mee personally explains each dish to diners. (📞020-364 25 60; www.grahamskitchen.amsterdam; Hemonystraat 38; lunch mains €12.50-17, 3-/4-/5-/6-course menus €38/47/56/62; ⏰6-10pm Tue & Wed, noon-2.30pm & 6-10pm Thu-Sat; 🚋4 Stadhouderskade)

Drinking

Watering Hole
CRAFT BEER

13 🚇 Map p108, B2

At this bare-brick space, the 30 taps feature a rotating range of brews such as New Zealand Yeastie Boys, Austrian Bevog, Spanish Naparbier and Amsterdam-brewed Two Chefs, alongside 45 bottled varieties. It's a fabulous place for gastropub fare (crab burgers, pork ribs with sage slaw). English-language pub quizzes take place on Monday. (www.thewatering-hole.nl; 1e Van der Helststraat 72; ⏱11.30am-1am Sun-Thu, to 3am Fri & Sat; 🛜; 🚊16/24 Albert Cuypstraat)

Brouwerij Troost
BREWERY

14 🚇 Map p108, B3

Watch beer being brewed in copper vats behind a glass wall at this outstanding craft brewery. Its dozen beers include a summery blonde, a smoked porter, a strong tripel and a deep-red Imperial IPA; it also distils cucumber and juniper gin from its beer and serves fantastic bar food, including crispy prawn tacos and humongous burgers. Book on weekend evenings. (📞020-760 58 20; www.brouwerijtroost.nl; Cornelis Troostplein 21; ⏱4pm-1am Mon-Thu, to 3am Fri, 2pm-3am Sat, to midnight Sun; 🛜; 🚊12 Cornelis Troostplein)

Twenty Third Bar
COCKTAIL BAR

15 🚇 Map p108, B4

High up in the skyscraping Hotel Okura Amsterdam (p175), Twenty Third Bar has sweeping views to the west and south, a stunning bar-snack menu prepared in the adjacent twin-Michelin-starred kitchen of **Ciel Bleu** (dishes €9-26, caviar €38-75 per 10g), champagne cocktails and Heineken on tap. (www.okura.nl; Hotel Okura Amsterdam, Ferdinand Bolstraat 333; ⏱6pm-1am Sun-Thu, to 2am Fri & Sat; 🚊12 Cornelius Troostplein)

Café Ruis
BAR

16 🚇 Map p108, C3

Opening to one of the liveliest terraces on plane tree–shaded local square Van der Helstplein, Café Ruis has a lounge-room-like interior with mismatched furniture, board games and a resident dog, Moe. Craft beers on tap include Amsterdam Brewboys' Amsterdam Pale Ale; Texelse Bierbrouwerij's Tripel, brewed on the Dutch island of Texel, is among the bottled options. (www.cafe-ruis.nl; Van der Helstplein 9; ⏱3pm-1am Mon-Thu, to 3am Fri, noon-3am Sat, to 1am Sun; 🛜; 🚊3 2e Van der Helstraat)

Blendbar
JUICE BAR

17 🚇 Map p108, B2

Alongside freshly squeezed juices and smoothies, this hole-in-the-wall place on busy Ferdinand Bolstraat also has protein shakes such as banana, whey, chocolate and oats, or espresso, cocoa fibre and raw cocoa. Yoghurt (in smoothies or served by itself with toppings such as goji berries) comes in skimmed, goat's-milk and soy varieties. (Ferdinand Bolstraat 21; ⏱8am-6pm Mon-Sat, noon-6pm Sun; 🚊16/24 Albert Cuypstraat)

Boca's

BAR

18 Map p108, B2

Boca's is the ultimate spot for *borrel* (drinks). Mezzanine seating overlooks the cushion-strewn interior, but in summer the best seats are on the terrace facing leafy Sarphatipark. Its pared-down wine list (seven by-the-glass choices) goes perfectly with its lavish sharing platters. (www.bar-bocas.nl; Sarphatipark 4; ☺10am-1am Mon-Thu, to 3am Fri & Sat, 11am-1am Sun; 🛜; 🚊3 2e Van der Helststraat)

Glouglou

WINE BAR

19 Map p108, C3

Natural, all-organic, additive-free wines are the stock-in-trade of this convivial wine bar in a rustic stained-glass-framed shop, where the party often spills into the street. More than 40 well-priced French wines are available by the glass; it also sells bottles to drink on site or take away. (http://glouglou.nl; 2e Van Der Helststraat 3; ☺5pm-midnight Mon-Thu, 4pm-1am Fri, 3pm-1am Sat, 3pm-midnight Sun; 🚊3 2e Van der Helststraat)

Gambrinus

BROWN CAFE

20 Map p108, B3

Named for legendary medieval European figure King Gambrinus, renowned for his love of beer, brewing and *joie de vivre*, this congenial split-level *café*, with giant windows and a sprawling terrace, is a local favourite. (www.gambrinus.nl; Ferdinand Bolstraat 180; ☺11am-1am Sun-Thu, to 3am Fri & Sat; 🛜; 🚊12 Cornelis Troostplein)

Café Berkhout

BROWN CAFE

21 Map p108, B1

With its dark wood, mirrored and chandelier-rich splendour and shabby elegance, this brown *café* is a natural post–Heineken Experience (p109) wind-down spot (it's right across the street). Great food includes house-speciality burgers. (www.cafeberkhout.nl; Stadhouderskade 77; ☺10am-1am Mon-Thu, to 3am Fri & Sat, 11am-1am Sun; 🛜; 🚊16/24 Stadhouderskade)

Entertainment

Rialto Cinema

CINEMA

22 Map p108, B3

This great old cinema near Sarphatipark focuses on premieres and shows eclectic art-house fare from around the world (foreign films feature Dutch subtitles). Three screens and a stylish on-site cafe. (☎020-676 87 00; www.rialtofilm.nl; Ceintuurbaan 338; adult/child from €10/7.50; 🚊3 2e Van der Helststraat)

Shopping

Hutspot

DESIGN

23 Map p108, C1

Named after the Dutch dish of boiled and mashed vegies, 'Hotchpotch' was founded with a mission to give young entrepreneurs the chance to sell their work. As a result, this concept store is an inspired mishmash of Dutch-designed furniture, furnishings, art, homewares and clothing plus a barber and a cool in-store cafe. (www.hutspot amsterdam.com; Van Woustraat 4; ⏱shop & cafe 10am-7pm Mon-Sat, noon-6pm Sun; 🛜; 🚊4 Stadhouderskade)

Good Genes
FASHION & ACCESSORIES

24 🔒 Map p108, A2

Premium fray-resistant selvedge denim is used by Good Genes' designers to create its seasonally themed collections, such as 1930s aviators. Designs are then sent to Italy to be made up; you can also get jeans custom made and returned to Amsterdam in around four days. The shop-studio occupies a pair of 19th-century warehouses that retain original industrial fittings. (http://thegoodgenes.com; Albert Cuypstraat 33-35; ⏱noon-6pm Mon, 11am-6pm Tue-Fri, 10am-5pm Sat; 🚊16/24 Albert Cuypstraat)

Charlie + Mary
FASHION & ACCESSORIES

25 🔒 Map p108, B2

This thoughtfully curated concept store sells ethical and sustainable labels, without compromising on style or fashion. Its selection of guilt-free products includes knitwear by Granny's Finest, wallets from O My Bag, do-it-yourself art by Soroche and some enticing chocolates. (📞020-662 8281; https://charliemary.com; Gerard Doustraat 84; ⏱1-6pm Mon, 10am-6pm Tue-Sat, noon-6pm Sun; 🚊16/24 Albert Cuypstraat)

Brick Lane
FASHION & ACCESSORIES

26 🔒 Map p108, B2

Individual, affordable designs arrive at this London-inspired boutique every

couple of weeks, keeping the selection up-to-the-minute. (www.bricklane-amster dam.nl; Gerard Doustraat 78; ⏱1-6pm Mon, 10.30am-6pm Tue-Sat, 12.30-5.30pm Sun; 🚊16/24 Albert Cuypstraat)

Van Beek
ART

27 🔒 Map p108, A1

If you're inspired by Amsterdam's masterpiece-filled galleries, street art and picturesque canalscapes, the De Pijp branch of this venerable Dutch art-supply shop is a great place to pick up canvases, brushes, oils, watercolours, pastels, charcoals and more. (www.vanbeekart.nl; Stadhouderskade 63-65; ⏱1-6pm Mon, 9am-6pm Tue-Fri, 10am-5pm Sat; 🚊16/24 Stadhouderskade)

't Kaasboertje
FOOD & DRINKS

28 🔒 Map p108, B2

Enormous wheels of Gouda line the walls of this enticing cheese shop, and more cheeses fill the glass display cabinet. Crispbreads and crackers are on hand, as well as reds, whites and rosés from the Netherlands, Belgium and Germany. (Gerard Doustraat 60; ⏱1-5.30pm Mon, 9am-5.30pm Tue-Fri, 9am-4pm Sat; 🚊16/24 Albert Cuypstraat)

Raak
CLOTHING

29 🔒 Map p108, B2

Unique casual clothing, bags, jewellery and homewares by Dutch and Scandinavian designers fill Raak's shelves and racks. (www.raakamsterdam.nl; 1e Van der Helststraat 46; ⏱noon-6pm Mon, 10am-6pm Tue-Sat; 🚊16/24 Albert Cuypstraat)

Explore

Oosterpark & East of the Amstel

Oost (East) is one of Amsterdam's most culturally diverse neighbour-hoods, a melting pot of Moroccan and Turkish enclaves. It's an area that grew up in the 19th century, with grand buildings and wide boulevards. The large English-style Oosterpark was laid out in 1861, while lush Flevopark, further east, dates from when this area was a country retreat.

The Sights in a Day

Spend the morning yodelling, sitting in yurts and checking out Dutch colonial booty at the **Tropenmuseum** (p118). Strike out east from here down 1e van Swindenstraat to find the **Dappermarkt** (p122), a fun cultural mix of people, food and wares mingling in the open air.

Continue east and the road eventually turns into Javastraat, where old Dutch fish shops and working-class bars sit adjacent to Moroccan and Turkish grocery stores. The exotic strip offers prime grazing, with some particularly outstanding bakeries. Assuming you're still hungry, keep going and you'll run into Javaplein for lunch at rustic **Wilde Zwijne** (p122). Or chill out nearby at the cafe of **Studio K** (p125).

Dinner in the greenhouse at **De Kas** (p122) is a one-of-a-kind meal; reserve ahead. Options abound for an evening drink: great views and clubby goings-on at **Canvas** (p124), or burgers and beer in the garden at **De Biertuin** (p125). Then again, you could always fritter away the night watching boats float on the Amstel at **De Ysbreeker** (p124).

 Top Sights

Tropenmuseum (p118)

Best of Amsterdam

Best Eating
De Kas (p122)

Roopram Roti (p124)

Best Parks & Gardens
Oosterpark (p122)

Getting There

🚊 **Tram** Tram 9 goes from the city centre to the Tropenmuseum. Trams 10 and 14 swing through the Oosterpark area on their east–west routes as well.

🚌 **Bus** No 757 starts at Amsterdam Centraal Station and stops near Oosterpark.

Ⓜ **Metro** The Wibautstraat stop is a stone's throw from the mod bars and hotels at the Oost's southwest edge.

Top Sights
Tropenmuseum

The gloriously quirky Tropenmuseum (Tropics Museum) has a whopping collection of ethnographic artefacts. Galleries surround a huge central hall across three floors and present exhibits with insight, imagination and lots of multimedia. The impressive arched building was built in 1926 to house the Royal Institute of the Tropics, and is still a leading research institute for tropical hygiene and agriculture.

Tropics Museum

👁 Map p120, D2

📞 0880 042 800

www.tropenmuseum.nl

Linnaeusstraat 2

adult/child €15/8

🕐 10am-5pm Tue-Sun

🚊 9/10/14 Alexanderplein

African mask, Tropenmuseum

Galleries

The Tropenmuseum galleries covering former Dutch colonies are particularly rich, with gorgeous Indonesian jewellery, shadow puppets, and waxworks and dioramas illustrating tropical life through history.

Downstairs, the 'World of Music' is a splendid exhibit, showing how music and instruments travel throughout the world, with hands-on exhibits and plenty of opportunities to listen.

There are also excellent temporary exhibits, which can range from body art to photographs of Aleppo.

Children's Museum

The museum has a small kids section, good for hands-on fun, with a shadow puppet theatre, the chance to construct with building blocks and other interactive exhibits.

Facilities

The museum's gift shop stocks enticing and unusual tropical arts and crafts.

With a superb terrace overlooking Oosterpark, the on-site restaurant, **De Tropen** (☎020-568 20 00; Linnaeusstraat 2; dishes €6-13; ⏱10am-6pm; 🚻; 🚊9 Swindenstraat), serves Indonesian, Indian and other global cuisines.

☑ Top Tips

▶ Get free admission to museum and exhibitions with the Museumkaart or I Amsterdam cards.

▶ Take your own headphones for the music exhibition (otherwise they're on sale for €1.50).

▶ The children's immersive exhibition ZieZo Marokko is only open at weekends, and you must reserve ahead for the English version.

✕ Take a Break

Across the road, **Louie Louie** (☎020-370 29 81; www.louielouie.nl; Linnaeusstraat 11; dishes €7-15; ⏱9am-1am Sun-Thu, to 3am Fri & Sat; 🚊Muiderpoort) serves laid-back brasserie food in a convivial setting, with a glass-covered terrace for all weathers.

A **B** **C** **D**

1

Nieuwe Keizersgracht
Nieuwe Keizersgr
PLANTAGE
Plantage Middenlaan
Artis Royal Zoo
Sarphatistr

Nieuwe Kerkstr
Plantage Muidergr
Plantage Muidergracht
Roetersstr

Nieuwe Prinsengracht
Nieuwe Prinsengr
Alexanderplein
Alexanderkade
22

Weesperstr
Nieuwe Achtergracht
Nieuwe Achtergr
Valckenierstr
Mauritskade
Tropenmuseum

2

Nieuwe Achtergracht
Valckenierstr
Sarphatistr
Spinozastr
's Gravesandestr

Weesper-plein
Valckenierstr
Sajetplein
M Zeldenruststr
Munten-damstr

M **Weesperplein**
Oosterpark
1

Rhijnspoor-plein

Oosterpark
De Schreeuw

3

Mauritskade
Slavery Memorial

Weesperzijde
Wibautstr
3.7

Ruyschstr
Onze Lieve Vrouwe Gasthuis
10
2e Oosterparkstr

3e Oosterparkstr

8
1e Oosterparkstr
OOSTERPARKBUURT
Populierenweg

4

7

Amstel
Weesperzijde

M **Wibautstraat**

9
G v Aemstelstr
Wibautstr

Amsteldijk

5

Nobelweg
3/

E
F
G
H

Mauritskade

Pieter Vlamingstr

Pontanusstr

Von Zesenstr

Dapperstr

Commelinstr

Timorplein

☆12 Borneostr

Bankastr

Madurastr

Sumatrastr

1

DAPPERBUURT

Javastr

Celebesstr

❌5

Balistr

INDISCHE
BUURT

Molukkenstr

Wagenaarstr

◉11 1e Van Swindenstr

◉2 Dappermarkt

Dapperplein

1e Atjehstr

2e Atjehstr

1e Atjehstr

Javaplein

❌6 2e Van Swindenstr

Riaowstr

2

Pieter Nieuwlandstr

Reinwardtstr

Insulindeweg

Molukkenstr

Wittenbachstr

🚇 Muiderpoort

Linnaeusstr

3

Polderweg

22.65

4

Middenweg

15

ⓝ 0 ————— 200 m
0 ————— 0.1 miles

Transvaalkade

TRANSVAALBUURT

59

Ringdijk

Kamerlingh Onneslaan

❌4

3◉
Park
Frankendael

For reviews see	
◉ Top Sights	p118
◉ Sights	p122
❌ Eating	p122
🍺 Drinking	p124
☆ Entertainment	p125

5

Sights

Oosterpark
PARK

1 Map p120, D2

The lush greenery of Oosterpark, with wild parakeets in the trees and herons stalking the large ponds, despite being laid out in English style, has an almost tropical richness in this diverse neighbourhood. It was established in 1891 as a pleasure park for the diamond traders who found their fortunes in the South African mines, and it still has an elegant, rambling feel. (⊘dawn-dusk; 🚼; 🚋9 1e Van Swindenstraat)

Dappermarkt
MARKET

2 ◉ Map p120, E2

The busy, untouristy Dappermarkt is a swirl of life and colour, with around 250 stalls. It reflects the Oost's diverse immigrant population, and is full of people (Africans, Turks, Dutch, hipsters), foods (apricots, olives, fish, Turkish kebabs) and goods from costume jewellery to cheap clothes, all sold from stalls lining the street. (www.dappermarkt.nl; Dapperstraat, btwn Mauritskade & Wijttenbachstraat; ⊘9am-5pm Mon-Sat; 🚋3/7 Dapperstraat)

Park Frankendael
PARK

3 ◉ Map p120, G5

These lovely, landscaped gardens are the grounds of a former country estate; the mansion, **Frankendael House** (www.huizefrankendael.nl; admission free; ⊘gardens dawn-dusk, house noon-5pm Sun; 🚋9 Hugo de Vrieslaan), is still standing and there are walking paths, flapping storks, decorative bridges and the remains of follies. (Middenweg 72; 🚋Middenweg 72)

Eating

De Kas
INTERNATIONAL €€€

4 ✕ Map p120, F5

In a row of stately greenhouses dating to 1926, De Kas has an organic attitude to match its chic glass greenhouse setting – try to visit during a thunderstorm! It grows most of its own herbs and produce right here and the result is incredibly pure flavours with innovative combinations. There's one set menu daily, based on whatever has been freshly harvested. Reserve in advance. (☎020-462 45 62; www.restaurantdekas.nl; Park Frankendael, Kamerlingh Onneslaan 3; lunch/dinner menu €39/49.50; ⊘noon-2pm & 6.30-10pm Mon-Fri, 6.30-10pm Sat; ✎; 🚋9 Hogeweg)

Wilde Zwijnen
DUTCH €€

5 ✕ Map p120, H1

The name means 'wild boar' and there's usually game on the menu in season at this modern Dutch restaurant. With pale walls and wood tables, the restaurant has a pared-down, rustic-industrial feel, and serves locally sourced, seasonal dishes with a creative twist. It's more of a meat-eater's paradise, but there's usually a vegetarian choice as well. (☎020-463

Understand
Amsterdam Today

Spreading Out
Amsterdam's cityscape has been a work-in-progress from the get-go. During the Golden Age, forward-thinking planners built the Canal Ring to drain and reclaim waterlogged land to accommodate the exploding population. Some four centuries later, Amsterdam is again running out of room – in 2016 alone, the city's population increased by 15,000, and it's expected to hit one million by the 2030s.

The shores along the IJ have seen swooping modern developments transforming industrial areas such as the Eastern Docklands and Western Docklands (on either side of Centraal Station). Across the water, the Amsterdam Noord area is also rapidly expanding.

Digging Down
Below ground, projects include the North–South metro line, aka the Noord/Zuidlijn, linking Amsterdam Noord with the World Trade Centre in the south. An extension and an East–West cross-city metro line are now on the drawing board.

Recent completions include a 600-space underground car and bicycle parking station below the Ruysdaelkade canal in De Pijp. In 2017 authorities approved plans to build an underground bicycle garage on the northern side of Centraal Station, which will provide parking for over 4000 bikes.

Ultimately, the goal is to build 50km of tunnels below the city centre with parking stations, sports facilities such as swimming pools, cinemas and supermarkets. Upon leaving Amsterdam's ring road, the A10, all traffic would be directed underground so that fumes are filtered before reaching the surface.

Starting Up
Amsterdam consistently ranks as one of the world's leading startup hubs, and has 1.3 startups per 1000 residents. Pioneering projects range from building a canal house and bridge by 3D printer to offering networks where residents can trade surplus green energy with each other.

30 43; www.wildezwijnen.com; Javaplein 23; mains €20, 3-/4-course menu €31.50/37.50; ⏱6-10pm Mon-Thu, noon-4pm & 6-10pm Fri-Sun, Eetbar from 5pm; 🛜; 🚊14 Javaplein)

Roopram Roti SOUTH AMERICAN €

6 🍴 Map p120, E2

This simple Surinamese cafe often has a queue out the door, but it moves fairly fast. Place your order at the bar – the scrumptiously punchy and flaky lamb roti 'extra' (with egg), and the *barra* (lentil doughnut) – and don't forget the fiery hot sauce. (1e Van Swindenstraat 4; mains €4-10; ⏱2-9pm Tue-Sun; 🚊9 1e Van Swindenstraat)

Eetcafe Ibis ETHIOPIAN €€

7 🍴 Map p120, A4

Bright with African art and brilliant-hued textiles, Ibis is a cosy and delightful spot to get your hands on

Local Life
Baking Lab
Baking workshops are offered for both adults and children at open bakery **Baking Lab** (Map p120, E3; 📞020-240 01 58; www.bakinglab.nl; Linnaeusstraat 99; 2hr workshop €20; ⏱9am-5pm Wed-Sat; 🚊3/7/9 Linnaeusstraat). You can make your own bread here, in the spirit of the idea of the old communal bakery, when people used to bring dough to knead and then put into the shared oven as few houses had ovens of their own.

(literally, using the spongy Ethiopian *injera* bread) herb-laced vegetable stews and spicy lamb and beef dishes; try the Ibis Special (meat or veg versions), which combines five dishes and bread. Ibis sells African beers to go with the authentic food. (📞020-692 62 67; www.eetcafeibis.com; Weesperzijde 43; mains €14-17; ⏱5-11pm Tue-Sun; 🛜; 🚊3 Wibautstraat/Ruyschstraat)

Drinking

De Ysbreeker BROWN CAFE

8 🚊 Map p120, A3

This historic but updated brown cafe first opened its doors in 1702, and is named after an icebreaker that used to dock in front to break the ice on the river during the winter months (stained-glass windows illustrate the scene). Inside, stylish drinkers hoist beverages in the plush booths and along the marble bar. (www.deysbreeker.nl; Weesperzijde 23; ⏱8am-1am Sun-Thu, to 2am Fri & Sat; 🛜; 🚊3 Wibautstraat/Ruyschstraat)

Canvas BAR

9 🚊 Map p120, B5

Zoom up to the Volkshotel's 7th floor (located in the former *Volkskrant* newspaper office) for the hotel bar (open to nonguests) with one of the best views in town. A creative-folk and hipster magnet, there are few better places for a beer or cocktails than this slice of urban cool. On weekend nights, it morphs into a fresh-beat dance club. (www.canvas7.nl; Wibautstraat 150; ⏱7am-1am Mon-Thu, to 4am Fri, 8am-4am Sat, to 1am Sun; Ⓜ Wibautstraat)

Bar Bukowski   BAR

10 🚾 Map p120, C3

Exuding bohemian cool in an emulation of its namesake, barfly writer Charles Bukowski, this cafe is a fine spot to linger under a cascade of greenery outside on sunny days, or in the art-deco interior when it's time to hunker down. Linger over a coffee, Heineken, banana milkshake or jasmine tea. Supplement with a baguette sandwich or *flammkuchen* (Alsatian thin-crust pizza). (☎020-370 16 85; www.barbukowski.nl; Oosterpark 10; ⏱8am-1am Mon-Thu, to 3am Fri, 9am-3am Sat, to 1am Sun; 🚌3/7 Beukenweg)

De Biertuin   BEER GARDEN

11 🚾 Map p120, E2

With a covered terrace, 'the beer garden' (with heaters for chillier weather) attracts a young and beautiful crowd of locals for the lengthy beer list (around 12 on tap and 50 more Dutch and Belgian varieties in the bottle) accompanied by simple but tasty food, such as burgers. (www.debiertuin.nl; Linnaeusstraat 29; ⏱11am-1am Sun-Thu, to 3am Fri & Sat; 🛜; 🚌9 1e Van Swindenstraat)

Ⓠ Local Life
Ajax

Amsterdam ArenA (www.amsterdamarena.nl; Arena Blvd 1; 🛜; Ⓜ Bijlmer ArenA) is a high-tech complex with a retractable roof and seating for 52,000 spectators. Four-times European champion Ajax, the Netherlands' most famous football team, play here. Football games usually take place on Saturday evenings and Sunday afternoons from August to May. Fans can also take a one-hour guided tour of the stadium (adult/child €14.50/9)

Entertainment

Studio K   CINEMA

12 ⭐ Map p120, G1

This hip Oost arts centre always has something going on, with two cinemas, a nightclub, a stage for bands and a theatre, an eclectic restaurant (serving sandwiches for lunch, and vegetarian-friendly, international-flavoured dishes for dinner) and a huge terrace. Stop in for a coffee and you might wind up staying all night to dance. (☎020-692 04 22; www.studio-k.nu; Timorplein 62; ⏱11am-1am Sun-Thu, to 3am Fri & Sat; 🛜; 🚌14 Zeeburgerdijk)

Explore

Nieuwmarkt, Plantage & the Eastern Islands

Buzzing Nieuwmarkt is sewn through with rich seams of history. Here is the Rembrandthuis – the master painter's studio – as well as centuries-old synagogues in the old Jewish quarter. Alongside is the leafy Plantage, with lots of greenery, and the sprawling zoo and botanical gardens. It segues into the Eastern Islands, home to former warehouses turned funkfest bars, and flagship modern Dutch architecture.

The Sights in a Day

☼ Begin at **Museum het Rembrandthuis** (p128; pictured left), the master's impressive home where he painted his finest works. For more history, visit the **Joods Historisch Museum** (p135), which provides the backstory to the neighbourhood's role as the old Jewish quarter. Then make your way to the Plantage. The **Artis Royal Zoo** (p134) wows the kids. The time-hewn plants of the **Hortus Botanicus** (p136) and the resistance exhibits of the **Verzetsmuseum** (p135) impress all ages.

☼ The former greenhouse containing **De Plantage** (p137) makes a stunning setting for lunch. Check out **NEMO** (p134), Amsterdam's kiddie-mobbed science centre. Continue along the waterfront to **ARCAM** (p136) to stock up on architectural info. Then plunge into **Het Scheepvaartmuseum** (p134), the treasure-rich maritime museum. When happy hour rolls around, stroll over to organic beermaker **Brouwerij 't IJ** (p138) and swill at the foot of an authentic windmill.

☾ Dine on contemporary Dutch cuisine at **Greetje** (p136) or **Gebr Hartering** (p137). Then take your pick of the *cafés* (pubs) around Nieuwmarkt square.

For a local's day in Nieuwmarkt and Plantage, see p130.

 Top Sights

Museum het Rembrandthuis (p128)

🔍 **Local Life**

Café-Hopping in Nieuwmarkt & Plantage (p130)

🖤 **Best of Amsterdam**

Best Drinking & Nightlife
De Sluyswacht (p140)

Best Shopping
Waterlooplein Flea Market (p131)

Hôtel Droog (p141)

Getting There

🚊 **Tram** Trams 9 and 14 go to Waterlooplein and the Jewish sights, as well as Plantage. Tram 10 goes to the Eastern Islands and Eastern Docklands.

Ⓜ **Metro** There are stops at Waterlooplein and Nieuwmarkt.

⛴ **Boat** Canal Bus stops are at Het Scheepvaartmuseum and near Amstel and Waterlooplein.

Top Sights
Museum het Rembrandthuis

The evocative Museum het Rembrandthuis provides an unparalleled insight into one of the Netherlands' greatest artistic geniuses, Rembrandt van Rijn. Set in the three-storey canal house where the artist lived at the height of his success, the interiors have been reconstructed according to a detailed inventory made when he had to leave the house after his fortunes took a dive.

Rembrandt House Museum

👁 Map p132, B3

☑ 020-520 04 00

www.rembrandthuis.nl

Jodenbreestraat 4

adult/child €13/4

🕙 10am-6pm

🚊 9/14 Waterlooplein

Rembrandt's studio

The House

The house dates from 1606. Rembrandt bought it for a fortune in 1639, made possible by his wealthy wife, Saskia van Uylenburgh. On the ground floor you'll see Rembrandt's living room/bedroom and the anteroom where he entertained clients.

Studio & Cabinet

Climb the narrow staircase and you'll come to Rembrandt's light-filled studio, laid out as though he's just nipped down to the kitchen for a bite to eat. Artists give demonstrations here on how Rembrandt sourced and mixed paints. Across the hall is Rembrandt's 'cabinet' – a mind-blowing room crammed with the curiosities he collected: seashells, glassware, Roman busts and stuffed alligators.

Etchings

The top floor is devoted to Rembrandt's famous etchings. The museum has a near-complete collection of them (about 250), although they're not all on display at once. Expect to see between 20 and 100 inky works at any one time, depending on the exhibition. Demonstrators crank up an oak press to show etching techniques several times daily.

Bankruptcy

The house ultimately caused Rembrandt's financial downfall. He was unable to pay off the mortgage, and in 1656 the household effects, artworks and curiosities were sold to compensate his creditors. It's thanks to the debt collector's itemised list that the museum has been able to reproduce the interior so authentically. Rembrandt lived the rest of his years in cheaper digs in the Jordaan.

☑ Top Tips

▶ It's worth taking part in one of the many engraving workshops.

▶ An interesting film about Rembrandt, presented by historian Simon Schama, plays in the basement.

▶ To avoid queues, book in advance online, or arrive early or late in the day.

✖ Take a Break

Linger over a canalside drink and snack at 17th-century charmer De Sluyswacht (p140), a charmingly wonky building right on the waterfront.

Local Life
Café-hopping in Nieuwmarkt & Plantage

Thanks to Nieuwmarkt's action-packed plaza and the Plantage's garden district greenery, the area makes for lively and lovely strolling. Distinctive *cafés* are the bonus here: they pop up in rustic shipping warehouses, 17th-century lock-keeper's quarters, the turreted city gate, and just about everywhere in between. A flea market and funky arts centre add to the daily buzz.

1 Fuel up at Café Scharrebier

Join locals reading the newspaper and playing Scrabble at **Café Scharrebier** (www.scharrebier.nl; Rapenburgerplein 1; ⏰11am-1am Sun-Thu, to 3am Fri & Sat; 🚌22 Kadijksplein). Overlooking the lock, the terrace at this snug little brown cafe is an inviting spot for a beer or sandwich. (Scharrebier, incidentally, was beer mixed with water to make it more affordable.)

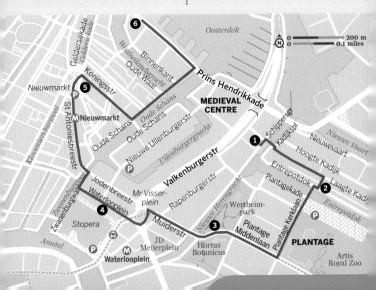

❷ Dockside at Entrepotdok

The Dutch East India Company, which grew rich on sea trade in the 17th century, owned **Entrepotdok** (🚊9/14 Plantage Kerklaan), a 500m row of warehouses that was the largest storage depot in Europe at the time. It's now packed with offices, apartments and dockside cafes perfect for lazing away a few hours at the water's edge.

❸ Wertheimpark's Memorial

Opposite the Hortus Botanicus, **Wertheimpark** (Plantage Parklaan; ⏰7am-9pm; 🚊9/14 Mr Visserplein) is a willow-shaded spot brilliant for lazing by the Nieuwe Herengracht. On the park's northeast side locals often place flowers at the Auschwitz Memorial, a panel of broken mirrors installed in the ground that reflects the sky.

❹ Flea Market Finds

Covering the square once known as Vlooienburg (Flea Town), the **Waterlooplein Flea Market** (www.waterlooplein. amsterdam; Waterlooplein; ⏰9.30am-6pm Mon-Sat; 🚊9/14 Waterlooplein) draws sharp-eyed customers seeking everything from antique knick-knacks to designer knock-offs and cheap bicycle locks. The street market started in 1880 when Jewish traders living in the neighbourhood started selling their wares here.

❺ Fondue at Café Bern

Indulge in a dipping frenzy at delightfully well-worn **Café Bern** (📞020-622 00 34; www.cafebern.com; Nieuwmarkt 9; mains €12-18; ⏰4pm-1am, kitchen 6-11pm; Ⓜ Nieuwmarkt). Locals have been flocking here for more than 30 years for the gruyère fondue and entrecôte (steak). The cafe closes for part of the summer, when steamy weather lessens the hot-cheese demand. Reservations advised.

❻ Scheepvaarthuis

Finish your walk on a high with a nose around the supreme example of the Amsterdam School, **Scheepvaarthuis** (Shipping House; Prins Hendrikkade 108; 🚊4/9/16/24 Centraal Station), with its nautical motifs, virtuoso stained glass and beautiful art-deco cafe.

A   B   C   D

1

Damrak

Damrak

22

20

OBA: Centrale
Bibliotheek Amsterdam 7 27
Oosterdokskade

Beurssstr

Warmoesstr

Lange
Niezel

Korte
Niezel

Zeedijk

Gelderskade

Gelderskade

Stormst

Binnen
Bantammerstr

Prins Hendrikkade

Oosterdok

2

Oudezijds Voorburgwal

Oudezijds Voorburgwal

Oudezijds Achterburgwal

Oudezijds Achterburgwal

Bloedstr

Barndest

Nieuw-
markt

26

18

Oude Waal

Binnenkant

Wadbeilandsgracht

NIEUWMARKT

Binnenkant

22.48

Koestr

25

30

31

Kezersstr

Koningsstr

Oude Schans

OudeSchans

14

Peperstr

Rapenburg

13

Bethaniënstr

Oude
Hoogstr

Nieuwmarkt

33

St Antonies-
breestr

Dijkstr

Oude Schans

Nieuwe Uilenburgerstr

Uilenburgergracht

Valkenburgerstr

Anne
Frankstr

3

Rusland

Kloveniersburgwal

Kloveniersburgwal

Nieuwe
Hoogstr

Zandstr

29

**Museum het
Rembrandthuis**

Raamgr

Ververstt

Staalkade

Groenburgwal

Zwanenburgwal

Zwanenburgwal

Jodenbreestr

12

Gassan
Diamonds

**MEDIEVAL
CENTRE**

Rapenburgerstr

Nieuwe-Heerengracht

Plantage
Parklaan

4

32 28

15

Staalstr

Waterlooplein

Stopera

23

Waterlooplein

Mr Visser-
plein

Nieuwe Amstelstr

6

Waterlooplein

Portuguese-
Israelite
Synagogue

8

Joods Historisch
Museum

JD Meijerplein

Muiderstr

Wertheim-
park

10

**Hortus
Botanicus**

Binnen
Amstel

Amstel

Amstelstr

Rembrandtplein

Blauwbrug

Hortusplantsoen

Nieuwe Herengr

Weesperstr

Nieuwe Keizersgr

Nieuwe Keizersgracht

Plantage

5

N

0   200 m
0   0.1 miles

Amstel

Amstel

Nieuwe Keizersgr

Nieuwe Kerkstr

E ⊕19

F ★24 Piet Heinkade **G** ▲ 17 **H**

Dijksgracht

IJ Tunnel 32,39

Naval Barracks

4◉ NEMO Science Museum

Historic Barges

Kattenburg

Kattenburgerstr

OOSTELIJKE EILANDEN

Wittenburg

Het Scheepvaart-museum ◉3

11🍷ARCAM

Kattenburgerplein

Schippersgr Kadijkspl

42

Kattenburgervaart

Nieuwevaart

Wittenburgerg

Grote Wittenburgerstr

Kleine Wittenburgerstr

Laagte Kadijk

Overhaalsgang

Oostenburgerg

Czaar Peterstr

Plantagekade

Entrepotdok

Entrepotdok

Hoogte Kadijk

Nieuwevaart

Verzets-museum Henri ●5 iaklaan

P

PLANTAGE

●1 Artis Royal Zoo

◉2 Micropia

✖16

ollandsche houwburg

Plantage Kerklaan

Plantage Middenlaan

Artis Royal Zoo

Sarphatistr

Alexanderkade

21 🛍

4

Mauritskade

Plantage Muiderg iidergracht

Artis Aquarium & Artis Zoological Museum

🍷22

5

Sights

Artis Royal Zoo   ZOO

1 Map p132, E4

A wonderfully leafy expanse, mainland Europe's oldest zoo has a fine range of wildlife, with extensive habitats and room to wander. A lovely stretch runs along the canal looking across to the old Entrepot dock. Habitats include African savannah and tropical rainforest, and there are reptiles, lions, jaguars, elephants, giraffes and lots of primates. There's also an aquarium complex featuring coral reefs, shark tanks and an Amsterdam canal displayed from a fish's point of view, plus a planetarium and kids' petting zoo. (☏020-523 34 00; www.artis.nl; Plantage Kerklaan 38-40; adult/child €20.50/17.50, incl Micropia €27/23; ☉9am-6pm Mar-Oct, to 5pm Nov-Feb; 🚊9/14 Plantage Kerklaan)

Micropia   MUSEUM

2 Map p132, E4

This is a germaphobe's nightmare. The fascinating invisible world is revealed at the world's first microbe museum. There are hands-on exhibits and microscopes to peer through and fascinating, if unsettling, facts about how many living organisms there are on everyday objects: do you keep a toothbrush as long as three months? It'll be host to seven million bacteria. There are also glass models of and information on viruses from ebola to smallpox. It's aimed at those aged eight and over. (www.micropia.nl; Artisplein, Plantage Kerklaan 38-40; adult/child €14/12, incl Artis Royal Zoo €28.50/24.50; ☉9am-6pm Sun-Wed, to 8pm Thu-Sat; 🚊9/14 Artis)

Het Scheepvaart-museum   MUSEUM

3 Map p132, E3

A waterfront 17th-century admiralty building houses this renovated, state-of-the-art presentation of maritime memorabilia. Highlights include exquisite and imaginatively presented Golden Age maps, fascinating 19th-century photo albums of early voyages and an audio-visual immersive journey evoking a voyage by ship. Outside you can also clamber over the full-scale replica of the Dutch East India Company's 700-tonne *Amsterdam,* one of the largest ships of the fleet, with its tiny bunks and sailors' hammocks, with the chance to mock fire cannons. (Maritime Museum; ☏020-523 22 22; www.hetscheepvaartmuseum.nl; Kattenburgerplein 1; adult/child €15/7.50; ☉9am-5pm; 👶; 🚊22/48 Kattenburgerplein)

NEMO Science Museum   MUSEUM

4 Map p132, E2

Perched atop the entrance to the IJ Tunnel is the unmissable slanted-roof green-copper building, designed by Italian architect Renzo Piano, almost surrounded by water. Its rooftop square has great views and water- and wind-operated hands-on exhibits. Inside, everything is interactive, with three floors of investigative mayhem. Experiment lifting yourself up via a pulley, making bubbles, building structures, dividing light into colours, racing your shadow and discovering the teenage mind. (☑020-531 32 33; www.nemosciencemuseum.nl; Oosterdok 2; €16.50, roof terrace free; ☺10am-5.30pm, closed Mon Sep-Mar, roof terrace to 9pm Jul & Aug; ☐22/48 IJ-Tunnel)

Verzetsmuseum
MUSEUM

 5 Map p132, E4

This museum brings the horror of German occupation in WWII vividly alive using letters, artifacts and personal stories to illuminate local resistance to (but also collaboration with) the Nazis. There's also a section on the Dutch East Indies (now Indonesia) pre- and postwar. Labels are in Dutch and English.Its **Verzetsmuseum Junior** relates the stories of four Dutch children, putting the resistance into context for kids. (Dutch Resistance Museum; ☑020-620 25 35; www.verzets museum.org; Plantage Kerklaan 61; adult/child €10/5; ☺10am-5pm Tue-Fri, from 11am Sat-Mon; ☐9/14 Plantage Kerklaan)

Joods Historisch Museum
MUSEUM

 6 Map p132, C4

The Joods Historisch Museum is a beautifully restored complex of four Ashkenazic synagogues from the 17th and 18th centuries. Displays show the rise of Jewish enterprise and its role in the Dutch economy, and the history of Jews in the Netherlands. An excellent audio tour is included and there's a small children's museum with

some activities. Tickets also include admission to the Portuguese-Israelite Synagogue and the Hollandsche Schouwburg (p136). (Jewish Historical Museum; ☑020-531 03 80; www.jhm.nl; Nieuwe Amstelstraat 1; adult/child €15/7.50; ☺11am-5pm; ☐9/14 Mr Visserplein)

OBA: Centrale Bibliotheek Amsterdam
LIBRARY

 7 Map p132, D1

This being Amsterdam, it has the funkiest library you can imagine, built in 2007 and spread over multiple light, bright floors. The basement is devoted to kids, and has a wigwam, a huge polar bear and the magical, marvelous Mouse Mansion, with 100 incredibly beautifully detailed rooms, the work of artist Karina Content. On the 7th floor is the reasonably priced cafe, with an outdoor terrace from where thrilling panoramic views roll across the water to Amsterdam's old town. (Amsterdam Central Library; ☑020-523 09 00; www.oba.nl; Oosterdok-skade 143; admission free; ☺10am-10pm; ☐4/9/16/24/26 Centraal)

Portuguese-Israelite Synagogue
SYNAGOGUE

8 Map p132, C4

With dizzying wooden barrel-vaulted ceilings, this was the largest synagogue in Europe when it was completed in 1675. It's still in use today, and has no electric light – after dark the candles in the vast chandeliers are lit for services. The large library belonging to the Ets

Haim seminary is one of the oldest and most important Jewish book collections in Europe. Outside (near the entrance) stairs lead underground to the treasure chambers to 16th-century manuscripts and gold-threaded tapestries. (www.portugesesynagoge.nl; Mr Visserplein 3; adult/child €15/7.50; ⏱10am-5pm Sun-Thu, to 4pm Fri, closed Sat Mar-Oct, reduced hours Nov-Feb; 🚊9/14 Mr Visserplein)

Hollandsche Schouwburg

MEMORIAL

9 Map p132, E4

Few theatres have had a history of such highs and lows. It was opened as the Artis Theatre in 1892 and became a hub of cultural life in Amsterdam, staging major dramas and operettas. In WWII the occupying Germans turned it into a Jew-only theatre, and later, horrifyingly, a detention centre for Jews held for deportation. (National Holocaust Museum; Holland Theatre; 📞020-531 03 10; www.hollandscheschouwburg.nl; Plantage Middenlaan 24; ⏱11am-5pm; 🚊9/14 Plantage Kerklaan)

Hortus Botanicus

GARDENS

10 Map p132, D4

A botanical garden since 1638, it bloomed as tropical seeds and plants were brought in (read: smuggled out of other countries) by Dutch trading ships. From here, coffee, pineapple, cinnamon and palm-oil plants were distributed throughout the world. The 4000-plus species are kept in wonderful structures, including the colonial-era seed house and a three-climate glasshouse. (Botanical Garden; www.dehortus.nl; Plantage Middenlaan 2a; adult/child €9/5; ⏱10am-5pm daily, to 7pm Jul & Aug; 🚊9/14 Mr Visserplein)

ARCAM

ARCHITECTURE

11 Map p132, E3

The Amsterdam Architecture Foundation is a striking waterside building hosting changing architectural exhibitions. (Stichting Architectuurcentrum Amsterdam; 📞020-620 48 78; www.arcam.nl; Prins Hendrikkade 600; admission free; ⏱1-5pm Tue-Sat; 🚊22/48 Kadijksplein)

Gassan Diamonds

FACTORY

12 Map p132, C3

See diamond cutters and polishers in action at this workshop. The free one-hour guided tour will prime you on assessing diamonds, then land you up in the shop with a chance to own your own sparklers, at a price. The factory sits on Uilenburg, one of the islands reclaimed in the 1580s during a sudden influx of Sephardic Jews from Spain and Portugal. In the 1880s Gassan became the first diamond factory to use steam power. (www.gassan.com; Nieuwe Uilenburgerstraat 173-175; admission free; ⏱9am-5pm; 🚊9/14 Waterlooplein)

Eating

Greetje

DUTCH €€€

13 Map p132, D3

Greetje is Amsterdam's most creative Dutch restaurant, using the best seasonal produce to resurrect and recreate traditional Dutch recipes, like pickled beef, braised veal with apricots and leek *stamppot* (traditional mashed potatoes and vegetables), and pork belly with Dutch mustard sauce. Kick off with the Big Beginning (€18), with a sampling of hot and cold starters. (📞020-779 74 50; www.restaurant greetje.nl; Peperstraat 23-25; mains €23-29; ⏰kitchen 6-10pm Sun-Thu, to 11pm Fri & Sat; 🚍22/34/35/48 Prins Hendrikkade)

Gebr Hartering
DUTCH €€

14 Map p132, D3

Lined in pale rustic wood, this gem was founded by two brothers, who offer either a la carte or a multi-course menu that changes daily according to the best seasonal produce available. A meal here is always a delight to linger over, so settle in and enjoy the accompanying wines and canalside location. (📞020-421 06 99; www.gebr-hartering.nl; Peperstraat 10; 5-/7-course menu €55/80, mains around €27.50; ⏰6-10.30pm Tue-Sun; 🚍32/33 Prins Hendrikkade)

Sterk Staaltje
DELI €

15 Map p132, A4

With pristine fruit and veg stacked up outside, Sterk Staaltje is worth entering just to breathe in the scent of the foodstuffs, with a fine range of ready-to-eat treats: Teriyaki meatballs, feta and sundried tomato quiche, pumpkin-stuffed wraps, a soup of the day and particularly fantastic sandwiches – roast beef, horseradish and *rucola* (arugula) or marinated chicken with guacamole and sour cream. (www.

sterkstaaltje.com; Staalstraat 12; dishes €4-7.60; ⏰8am-7pm Mon-Fri, 8am-6pm Sat, 11am-5pm Sun; 🚍4/9/14/16/24 Muntplein)

De Plantage
MODERN EUROPEAN €€

16 Map p132, E4

Huge and graceful, this is an impressive space in a 1870s-builtformer greenhouse decked with blonde wood and black chairs, with hothouse views of strutting geese in the Artis Royal Zoo's grounds (p134). Food is creative, and tasty, if not outstanding, with dishes like salad with roasted octopus, couscous, fennel, *bacalau* (dried and salted cod), mussels and saffron mayo. (📞020-760 68 00; www.caferestaurantde plantage.nl; Plantage Kerklaan 36; mains lunch €7.50-21.50, dinner €15.50-21.50; ⏰9am-1am Mon-Fri, 10am-1am Sat & Sun, kitchen closes 10pm; 🚍9/14 Plantage Kerklaan)

De Kleine Kaart
INTERNATIONAL €€

17 Map p132, G1

The 'Small Menu' is a charming little neighbourhood restaurant with an idyllic view of boats bobbing on the water. Its small tables, adorned by fresh flowers, are where you can tuck into fresh, simple pleasures, such as steak, hamburgers and salad bowls. (📞020-354 78 38; www.dekleinekaart.nl; Piraeusplein 59; mains €15-19; ⏰noon-9pm Tue-Sun; 🚍10 Azartplein)

Hemelse Modder
DUTCH €€

18 Map p132, C2

'Heavenly Mud', named after its signature dark and white chocolate mousse, has blonde-wood tables and a Dutch-meets-global menu that emphasises North Sea fish and farm-fresh produce, with dishes like pan-fried fillet of North Sea plaice with capers, cream, mashed potatoes, samphire and sea aster. There's a lovely terrace for when the sun comes out. (📞020-624 32 03; www.hemelsemodder.nl; Oude Waal 11; 3-/4-/5-course menu €36/43/49; ⏰6-11pm daily, plus noon-2.30pm Sat & Sun; Ⓜ Nieuwmarkt)

Drinking

Hannekes Boom BEER GARDEN

19 Map p132, E1

Reachable via a couple of pedestrian/bike bridges from NEMO, this nonchalantly cool, laid-back waterside *café* built from recycled materials has a beer garden that really feels like a garden, with timber benches, picnic tables under the trees and a hipster, arty crowd enjoying sitting out in the sunshine (it comes into its own in summer). (www.hannekesboom.nl; Dijksgracht 4; ⏰10am-1am Sun-Thu, to 3am Fri & Sat; 🚊26 Muziekgebouw)

SkyLounge COCKTAIL BAR

20 Map p132, C1

With wow-factor views whatever the weather, this bar offers a 360-degree panorama of Amsterdam from the 11th floor of the DoubleTree Amsterdam Centraal Station hotel – and just gets better when you head out to its vast, sofa-strewn SkyTerrace, with an outdoor bar. To toast the view: a choice of 500 different cocktails; DJs regularly hit the decks. (www.skyloungeamsterdam.com; Oosterdoksstraat 4; ⏰11am-1am Sun-Tue, to 2am Wed & Thu, to 3am Fri & Sat; 🚊1/2/4/5/9/14/16/24 Centraal Station)

Brouwerij 't IJ BREWERY

21 Map p132, H4

Can you get more Dutch than drinking an organic beer beneath the creaking sails of the 1725-built De Gooyer Windmill? This is Amsterdam's leading organic microbrewery with delicious standard, seasonal and limited-edition brews; try the fragrant, hoppy house brew, Plzeň. There's the tiled tasting room, lined by an amazing bottle collection, or the plane tree–shaded terrace. (www.brouwerijhetij.nl; Funenkade 7; ⏰brewery

---

Ⓠ Local Life

Tokoman

Queue with the folks getting their Surinamese spice on at **Tokoman** (Map p132, B4; Waterlooplein 327; sandwiches €3-4.50, dishes €6.50-13.50; ⏰11am-8pm Mon-Sat; 🚊9/14 Waterlooplein). It makes a sensational *broodje pom* (a sandwich filled with a tasty mash of chicken and a starchy Surinamese tuber). You'll want the *zuur* (pickled-cabbage relish) and *peper* (chilli) on it, plus a cold can of coconut water to wash it down.

Hôtel Droog (p141)

2-8pm, English tour 3.30pm Fri-Sun; 10 Hoogte Kadijk)

De Groene Olifant   BROWN CAFE

22 Map p132, G5

A local favourite for generations, inside the Green Elephant is all 19th-century opulence with wrought-iron chandeliers, intricate woodwork and dim lighting, a setting for a drink back in time. Sit at the circa-1880 bar and admire the art deco glass, retreat to the lofted dining room for dinner like previous elegant Plantage residents or catch some rays at the outside tables. (www.degroeneolifant.nl; Sarphatistraat 510; 11am-1am Sun-Thu, to 2am Fri & Sat; 9 Alexanderplein)

Entertainment

Muziektheater   CLASSICAL MUSIC

23 ⭐ Map p132, B4

The Muziektheater is home to the Netherlands Opera and the National Ballet, with some spectacular performances. Big-name performers and international dance troupes also take the stage here. Free classical concerts (12.30pm to 1pm) are held most Tuesdays from September to May in its Boekmanzaal. (☏020-625 54 55; www.operaballet.nl; Waterlooplein 22; ⏰box office noon-6pm Mon-Fri, to 3pm Sat & Sun or until performance Sep-Jul; 9/14 Waterlooplein)

Understand
Tilted Architecture

No, you're not drunk... Amsterdam's buildings are leaning. Some – like **De Sluyswacht** (Map p132, B3; www.sluyswacht.nl; Jodenbreestraat 1; ⊙noon-1am Sun-Thu, to 3am Fri & Sat; 🚊9/14 Waterlooplein) – have shifted over the centuries, but many canal houses were deliberately constructed to tip forward. Interior staircases were narrow, so owners needed an easy way to move large goods and furniture to the upper floors. The solution: a hoist built into the gable, to lift objects up and in through the windows. The tilt allows loading without bumping into the house front.

Muziekgebouw aan 't IJ
CONCERT VENUE

24 ⭐ Map p132, G1

A dramatic glass-and-steel box on the IJ waterfront, this multidisciplinary performing-arts venue has a state-of-the-art main hall with flexible stage layout and great acoustics. Its jazz stage, **Bimhuis** (🕿020-788 21 88; www.bimhuis.nl; Piet Heinkade 3; tickets free-€32), is more intimate. Try the Last Minute Ticket Shop (www.lastminuteticketshop.nl) for discounts. (🕿tickets 020-788 20 00; www.muziekgebouw.nl; Piet Heinkade 1; tickets free-€40; ⊙box office noon-6pm; 🚊26 Muziekgebouw)

Bethaniënklooster
CLASSICAL MUSIC

25 ⭐ Map p132, A2

This former monastery near Nieuwmarkt has a glorious ballroom, and is a superb place to take in exceptional chamber music. Jazz fills the vaulted basement cellar. (🕿020-625 00 78; Barndesteeg 6b; ⊙Sep-Jul; Ⓜ Nieuwmarkt)

Amsterdams Marionetten Theater
THEATRE

26 ⭐ Map p132, B2

An enchanting enterprise that seems to exist in another era, in a former blacksmith's shop this marionette theatre presents fairy tales or Mozart operas, such as *The Magic Flute,* but kids and adults alike are just as enthralled by the magical stage sets, period costumes and beautiful singing voices that bring the diminutive cast to life. (🕿020-620 80 27; www.marionetten theater.nl; Nieuwe Jonkerstraat 8; adult/child €15/7.50, 1.5hr tour €15; Ⓜ Nieuwmarkt)

Conservatorium van Amsterdam
CLASSICAL MUSIC

27 ⭐ Map p132, D1

Catch a classical recital by students at the Netherlands' largest conservatory of music. There are regular festivals in this snazzy contemporary building with state-of-the-art acoustics. (🕿020-527 78 37; www.ahk.nl/conservatorium; Oosterdokskade 151; 🚊4/9/16/24 Centraal Station)

Shopping

Hôtel Droog
DESIGN, HOMEWARES

28 🔒 Map p132, A4

Not a hotel, but a local design house, Droog means 'dry' in Dutch, and these products are full of dry wit. You'll find all kinds of stylish versions of useful things – a chic dish sponge or streamlined hot water bottle – as well as the kind of clothing that should probably by law be worn by a designer or an architect. (www.droog.com; Staalstraat 7; ⏰9am-7pm; 🚊4/9/14/16/24 Muntplein)

Knuffels
TOYS, SHOES

29 🔒 Map p132, B3

Bobbing mobiles and suspended toys have a motor and strings keeping them in fascinating constant motion in the window of this busy toyshop. There are plenty of *knuffels* (soft cuddly toys), puppets, teddies and jigsaw puzzles. (www.knuffels.com; St Antoniesbreestraat 39-51; ⏰10am-6pm Mon-Sat, from 11am Sun; 🚹; Ⓜ Nieuwmarkt)

Antiques Market
MARKET

30 🔒 Map p132, B2

Treasure hunters will find lots of old books and bric-a-brac to peruse. (Nieuwmarkt; ⏰9am-5pm Sun May-Sep; Ⓜ Nieuwmarkt)

Boerenmarkt
MARKET

31 🔒 Map p132, B2

Stalls selling organic foods and produce draw crowds on Saturdays.

(Farmers Market; Nieuwmarkt; ⏰9am-4pm Sat; Ⓜ Nieuwmarkt)

Juggle
TOYS

32 🔒 Map p132, A4

Wee Juggle puts more than mere balls in the air: it also sells circus supplies, from unicycles to fire hoops to magic tricks. (www.juggle-store.com; Staalstraat 3; ⏰noon-5.30pm Tue-Sat; 🚊4/9/14/16/24 Muntplein)

Joe's Vliegerwinkel
TOYS

33 🔒 Map p132, B3

Kids and grown ups will appreciate this specialised kite shop, which also sells lots of other random quirk, from solar-power hula dancers to lantern fairylights. You can also buy build-it-yourself kits. (www.joesvliegerwinkel.nl; Nieuwe Hoogstraat 19; ⏰noon-6pm Tue-Fri, to 5pm Sat; 🚹; Ⓜ Nieuwmarkt)

Local Life
Amsterdam Roest

The once derelict shipyards now hosts an epically cool artist collective-bar-restaurant. **Amsterdam Roest** (www.amsterdamroest.nl; Jacob Bontiusplaats 1; ⏰noon-1am Sun-Thu, to 3pm Fri & Sat; 🚊22 Wittenburgergracht). It has a canalside terrace, mammoth playground of ropes and tyres, hammocks, street art, a sandy beach in summer and bonfires in winter.

Explore

Amsterdam Noord

Long neglected, Amsterdam Noord has been reinvented as the city's hippest neighbourhood. This area across the IJ River from central Amsterdam encompasses ex-industrial areas, cutting-edge architecture and hangars turned hipster hang-outs where the walls burst with street art, minutes away from fields, horses and windmills.

DENNIS VAN DE WATER/SHUTTERSTOCK ©

The Sights in a Day

☀ Begin at **NDSM-werf** (p145). This former shipbuilding yard was an important industrial area that fell into disuse from the 1980s, before squatters filled the void. Today it has striking modernist architecture, a hangar full of artists' studios and an ex-USSR **submarine** (p146) in the harbour. Numerous cool waterside restaurants here are ideal for lunch; try **Hangar** (p148) for fab burgers.

☀ From NDSM-werf it's a five- to 10-minute bike ride to the **A'Dam Tower** (p145) and the **Eye Film Institute** (p146; pictured left). Further along the riverbank to the east are more waterside bars and restaurants, and the enchantingly pretty dike, **Nieuwendammerdijk** (p146). Cycle routes fan out into the countryside; from here you can explore the lakes and _polder_ (area of drained land) to the north.

☾ Come evening, return to NDSM-werf for dinner and drinks at **Pllek** (p147) before checking out the club events at **Sexyland** (p146; the founders were originally planning to open in a former porn cinema in central Amsterdam, hence the name, but instead found this long low hut that once served as barracks).

 Best of Amsterdam

Best Drinking & Nightlife
Oedipus Brewery & Tap Room (p148)

Best For Free
Kunststad (Art City; p146)

EYE Film Institute (p146)

Best Entertainment
EYE Film Institute (p146)

Getting There

🚢 **Boat** Free 24-hour ferries run between Amsterdam Centraal Station, Buiksloterweg, NDSM-werf and IJplein.

🚲 **Bike** You can take bikes over on the ferry, or hire bikes locally.

Ⓜ **Metro** From mid-2018 Amsterdam's new metro line adds a link to the Noord.

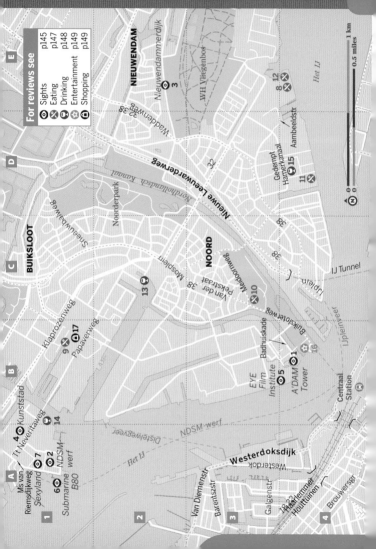

For reviews see
- ◎ Sights   p145
- ⊗ Eating   p147
- ◐ Drinking   p148
- ✪ Entertainment   p149
- ◎ Shopping   p149

NIEUWENDAM

BUIKSLOOT

NOORD

EYE Film Institute

A'DAM Tower

Centraal Station

NDSM-werf

Westerdoksdijk

0.5 miles

1 km

NDSM-werf

Sights

A'DAM Tower

NOTABLE BUILDING

1 ⊙ Map p144, B4

The 22-storey A'DAM Tower used to be the Royal Dutch Shell oil company offices, but has been funked up to become Amsterdam's newest big attraction. Take the trippy lift to the rooftop for awe-inspiring views in all directions, with a giant four-person swing that kicks out over the edge for those who have a head for heights (you're well secured and strapped in). (www.adamtoren.nl; Overhoeksplein 1; Lookout adult/child €12.50/6.50, premium €15/7.50, family ticket min 3 people €10/5; ⊙Lookout 10am-10pm; 🚢Badhuiskade)

NDSM-werf

AREA

2 ⊙ Map p144, A1

NDSM-werf is a derelict shipyard turned edgy arts community 15 minutes upriver from the city centre. It wafts a post-apocalyptic vibe: an old submarine slumps in the harbour, abandoned trams rust by the water's edge, and graffiti splashes across almost every surface. Young creatives hang out at the smattering of cool cafes. The area is a centre for underground culture and events, such as the **Over het IJ Festival** (www.overhetij.nl; ⊙early Jul). Hip businesses like MTV and Red Bull have their European headquarters here. (www.ndsm.nl; 🚢NDSM-werf)

MAREANDMARE/GETTY IMAGES ©

Nieuwendammerdijk   AREA

3 ◉ Map p144, E2

Enchanting chocolate-box prettiness
characterises this long, narrow street
of wooden Dutch houses, now prime
real estate, with hollyhocks nodding
beside every porch. Many houses date
from the 1500s, and numbers 202
to 204 were where the shipbuilding
family De Vries-Lentsh lived. Numbers
301 to 309 were once captains' houses.
(🚏Badhuiskade)

Kunststad   ART STUDIO

4 ◉ Map p144, B1

This former shipbuilding warehouse
is filled with artists' studios, with
175 artists working in the NDSM
broedplaats (breeding ground). It's a
big enough space that you can cycle
or walk around the area, with huge
artworks hanging from the ceiling,
and structures within the hangar. (Art
City; 🚏NDSM-werf)

EYE Film Institute   MUSEUM, CINEMA

5 ◉ Map p144, B4

At this modernist architectural
triumph that seems to balance on
its edge on the banks of the IJ (also
pronounced 'eye') River, the institute
screens movies from the 40,000-title
archive in four theatres, sometimes
with live music. Exhibits (€9 to €15)
of costumes, digital art and other
cinephile amusements run in conjunc-
tion with what's playing. A view-tastic
bar-restaurant with a fabulously
sunny terrace (when the sun makes
an appearance) is a popular hang-out
on this side of the river. EYE does not
accept cash; you must use a credit or
debit card. (📞020-589 14 00; www.eyefilm.
nl; IJpromenade 1; ⏰10am-7pm Sat-Thu, to
9pm Fri; 🚏Buiksloterweg)

Submarine B-80   SUBMARINE

6 ◉ Map p144, A1

Soviet Project 611 submarine B-80
dates from 1952, and was built in
Severodvinsk, Russia. It was moored
previously in the Dutch Navy port
of Den Helder in North Holland, but
was brought to Amsterdam. It had its
interior stripped as the owners hoped
to rent it as a party venue, but it now
lies as an empty, if visually arresting,
shell in the harbour. (NDSM Harbour;
🚏NDSM-werf)

Sexyland   ARTS CENTRE

7 ◉ Map p144, A1

See the neon sign and you'll be
forgiven for thinking this is an
outpost of the Red Light District. But
Sexyland is a members' club that has
365 co-owners, each of whom puts on
an annual event. This can range from
ping-pong to tantric tango, with club
nights at weekends; the public can
attend any of the activities during that
week by buying a week-long membership. (www.sexyland.amsterdam; Ms van
Riemsdijkweg 39; weekly membership €2.50,
admission dependent on event; ⏰hours vary;
🚏NDSM-werf)

Eating

Hotel de Goudfazant   FRENCH €€€

 8   Map p144, E4

With a name taken from lyrics of the Jacques Brel song 'Les Bourgeois', this extraordinary gourmet hipster restaurant spreads through a cavernous former garage, still raw and industrial, and sticks to the theme by having cars parked inside. Rockstar-looking chefs cook up a French-influenced storm in the open kitchen. There is no hotel, FYI, except in name. (☏020-636 51 70; www.hoteldegoudfazant.nl; Aambeeldstraat 10h; 3-course menu €32; ☺6pm-1am Tue-Sun; ☒32/33 Johan van Hasseltweg, ☖IJplein)

Waargenoegen   CAFE €

9   Map p144, B1

This hippy-feeling cafe in a container behind two large vintage stores, Neef Louis and Van Dijk and Ko, serves deliciously good toasties and a particularly fantastic apple tart. (Papaverweg 46; snacks €4-6; ☺10am-4pm Tue-Fri, to 5pm Sat, 11am-5pm Sun; ♿; ☖NDSM-werf)

Cafe Modern   ITALIAN €€

10   Map p144, C3

Amid artful yet simple decor with a mid-century feel, Cafe Modern is serious about its gastronomy and is a good-value option for fine cooking, with lots of veggie choices using fresh seasonal ingredients for dishes like artichoke with walnut, saffron risotto or

broad beans with burrata. (Meidoornweg 2; 4-course menu €40, mains €12-16; ☺from 6pm Mon-Sat; ☖Buiksloterweg)

Cafe-Restaurant Stork   SEAFOOD €€

11   Map p144, D4

A sometime factory on the IJ River, this huge place has a dramatically soaring interior and a cool terrace shaded with sails on the waterfront. It feels right that Stork should specialise in fish and seafood (though there are a few veggie and meat dishes too), serving especially good crab as well as other crustaceans and fresh fish of the day. (☏020-634 40 00; Gedempt Hamerkanaal 201; lunch €9-17, dinner €14-22; ☺11am-late daily Apr-Sep, Tue-Sun Oct-Mar; ☖IJplein)

Hangar
RESTAURANT €€

12 Map p144, E4

A restaurant, in a...hangar, this relaxing choice is on the water's edge, with a great deck and laid-back music, giving it a beachy vibe. Food includes dishes such as crunchy Ottolenghi salads, succulent burgers and steaks. (📞020-363 86 57; Aambeeldstraat 36; snacks & mains €13-24; ⏱10am-1am Mon-Thu, to 3am Fri & Sat, to midnight Sun; ⛴IJplein)

Drinking

Café de Ceuvel
BAR

13 Map p144, C2

The inspiring Café de Ceuvel is tucked in a former shipyard. Designed by architect Wouter Valkenier and built from recycled materials, this waterside spot is a surprising oasis alongside the canal and built out onto

---

Top Tip

Cycling in Amsterdam Noord

The best way to explore Noord is via bike. Places are spread out, there isn't much traffic and there are lots of cycle routes. You can take bikes on the free ferries, or hire one on the Noord side through **Orangebike** (Map p144, B4; 📞06 4684 2083; www.orange-bike.nl; Buiksloterweg 5c; tours €22.50-37.50, hire per hr/day from €5/11; ⏱9am-6pm; ⛴Buiksloterweg).

---

an island. Drinks include homemade ginger lemonade, plus bottled beer from local heroes Oedipus Brewery. (📞020-229 62 10; www.deceuvel.nl; Korte Papaverweg 4; ⏱11am-midnight Tue-Thu & Sun, to 2am Fri & Sat; 🚌34/35)

Café Noorderlicht
BAR

14 Map p144, B1

The original Café Noorderlicht was in a boat, which burned down. Safely ensconced in a soaring flag-draped greenhouse, with grassy waterside lawns outside and a mini-stage, it now has a pub-garden-meets-festival vibe. There's a big play area outside, with a tin rocket to climb on, so it's good for families. Food, craft beers and lots of other drinks are on the menu. (www.noorderlichtcafe.nl; NDSM-plein 102; ⏱11am-10pm, closed Mon in winter; ⛴NDSM-werf)

Oedipus Brewery & Tap Room
BREWERY

15 Map p144, D4

Oedipus began with four friends trying out some experimental brewing methods, and its bright-labelled bottles are now an Amsterdam institution. This funky warehouse space is a key Noord hang-out, with outdoor seating lit by coloured fairy lights. Immerse yourself in some Oedipus history by sampling Mannenliefde 'Men Love', their first-ever beer, still going strong (not too strong, at 6%). (www.oedipus.com; Gedempt Hamerkanaal 85; ⏱5-10pm Thu, 2-11pm Fri & Sat, 2-10pm Sun; ⛴IJplein)

Oedipus Brewery & Tap Room

Entertainment

Tolhuistuin   LIVE PERFORMANCE

16 ⭐ Map p144, B4

In what was the former Shell workers' canteen for 70 years from 1941, the nifty Tolhuistuin arts centre hosts African dance troupes, grime DJs and much more on its garden stage under twinkling lights, and also houses club nights in its Paradiso nightclub. (www.tolhuistuin.nl; IJpromenade 2; ⏱10am-10pm; 🚢Buiksloterweg)

Shopping

Neef Louis Design   VINTAGE

17 🔒 Map p144, B1

A huge warehouse full of vintage, designer and industrial furniture, this is a treasure trove of lamps made out of books, pop-art chairs, mid-century bookcases, antique clay pipes, neon signs and much, much more. There's a cafe on-site. (www.neeflouis.nl; Papaverweg 46; ⏱10am-6pm; 🚢NDSM-werf)

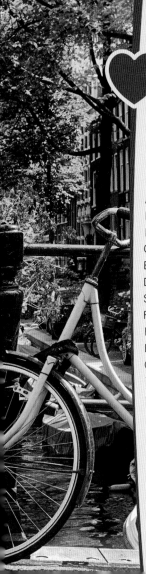

The Best of
Amsterdam

Canalside view
TUNART/GETTY IMAGES ©

Best Walks
Amsterdam's Splashiest Canals

🏃 The Walk

More canals flow in Amsterdam than in Venice. Get the camera ready, because this walk passes some of the city's most beautiful waterways. They're more than just a pretty picture, though. For more than four centuries the canals have performed the epic task of keeping Amsterdam above water, since they help help drain the soggy landscape. Today 100km of channels do their duty. The romantic backdrops and groovy places to float a boat are a lucky bonus.

Start Corner of Staalstraat and Groenburgwal; 🚋4/9/14/16/24 Muntplein

Finish De Ysbreeker; 🚋 3 Wibautstraat/Ruyschstraat

Length 3km; two hours with dawdling

🍴 Take a Break

Sip coffee mid the vintage-thrift decor at **Café Langereis** (www.cafelangereis.nl; Amstel 202; ⏱11am-3am Sun-Thu, to 4am Fri & Sat; 🛜; 🚋4/9/14 Rembrandtplein), at the foot of the Blauwbrug (Blue Bridge).

Groenburgwal

❶ Groenburgwal

Step out onto the white drawbridge that crosses the **Groenburgwal** and look north. Many Amsterdammers swear this is the loveliest canal view of all – a pick backed by Impressionist Claude Monet, who painted it in 1874 as *The Zuiderkerk (South Church) at Amsterdam: Looking up the Groenburgwal.*

❷ Stopera

Head to the **Stopera** building, Amsterdam's combination of city hall and Muziektheater (p139). Its terrace is a great place for sitting and watching the boats go by on the Amstel

❸ Blauwbrug

Cross the river via the 1884 **Blauwbrug** (Blue Bridge). Inspired by Paris' Alexander III bridge, it features tall, ornate street lamps topped by the imperial crown of Amsterdam, fish sculptures, and foundations shaped like a medieval ship prow.

➍ Reguliersgracht

Walk along the Herengracht to **Reguliersgracht** (p82), the 'seven bridges' canal. Stand with your back to the Thorbeckeplein and the Herengracht flowing directly in front of you. Lean over the bridge and sigh at the seven humpbacked arches leading down the canal straight ahead.

➎ Magere Brug

Walk along the Keizersgracht and turn right towards the wedding-photo-favourite **Magere Brug** (Skinny Bridge). According to legend, two sisters built it. They lived on opposite sides of the river and wanted an easy way to visit each other. Alas, they only had enough money to construct a narrow bridge.

➏ Amstelsluizen

Continue south to the **Amstelsluizen**. These impressive locks, dating from 1674, allow the canals to be flushed with fresh water. The sluices on the city's west side are left open as

the stagnant water is pumped out to sea.

➐ De Ysbreeker

Cross the river once more; take Prof Tulpplein past the InterContinental hotel to **De Ysbreeker** (p124). The

building used to be an inn for the tough guys who broke ice on the Amstel so boats could pass. Grab a seat on the enormous waterfront terrace to see what's gliding by these days.

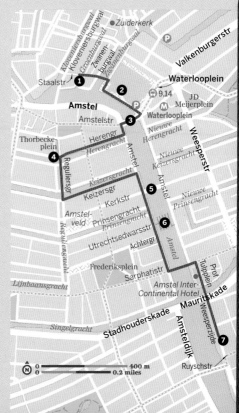

Best Walks
Cheese, Gin & Monuments

🏃 The Walk

This tour is a hit parade of Amsterdam's favourite foods and historic sights. Swoop through the Western Canals and City Centre, gobbling up traditional *kaas* (cheese), *haring* (herring) and *jenever* (gin) in between stops at the city's birthplace, its Royal Palace and a Golden Age art cache. It's a big bite of Amsterdam in under two hours. The best time to trek is early afternoon, when opening times for the sights and bars coincide.

Start De Kaaskamer; 🚊 1/2/5 Spui

Finish Wynand Fockink; 🚊 4/9/16/24 Dam

Length 2km, 1½ to two hours with stops

✕ Take a Break

Inviting cafes and brainy bookstores ring the Spui (pronounced 'spow'; rhymes with 'now'), a broad square where academics and journalists hang out. **Hoppe** (p37) has poured for the literati for over 340 years.

Dutch cheese

❶ De Kaaskamer

The Dutch eat more than 14kg of cheese per person annually and it appears much of that hunky goodness is sold right here in **De Kaaskamer** (p60). Wheels of Gouda, Edam and other locally made types stack up to the rafters. Get a wedge to go.

❷ Begijnhof

On the Spui, just past the American Book Center, is a humble wood door. Push it open and behold the hidden community known as the **Begijnhof** (p26) surrounding two historic churches and gardens. Cross the courtyard to the other entrance.

❸ Civic Guard Gallery

From the Begijnhof turn north and walk a short distance to the **Civic Guard Gallery** (p32). Paintings of stern folks in ruffled collars stare down from the walls. Cross the gallery and depart through the Amsterdam Museum's courtyard restaurant onto Kalverstraat.

MICHAEL LUHRENBERG/GETTY IMAGES ©

4 Royal Palace

Kalverstraat deposits you by the **Royal Palace** (p24), King Willem-Alexander's pad, though he's rarely here, preferring Den Haag for his digs. The sumptuous interior deserves a look.

5 Nieuwe Kerk

The palace's neighbour is the **Nieuwe Kerk** (p30), the stage for Dutch coronations. After admiring its mightiness, get onto crowded Nieuwendijk, which you'll walk for a short while until you dive down Zoutsteeg.

6 Rob Wigboldus Vishandel

C'mon, stop being shy about eating raw fish. Try the famed Dutch herring at **Rob Wigboldus Vishandel** (p34), a teeny three-table shop. Once sated, depart Zoutsteeg onto Damrak.

7 Dam

Cross Damrak so you're on the Nationaal Monument side of the **Dam** (p31) – Amsterdam's birthplace. Wade through the sea of bikes to see the urns behind the monument, which hold earth from East Indies war cemeteries. Now follow the street leading behind the NH Grand Hotel Krasnapolsky.

8 Wynand Fockink

'Sshh, the *jenever* is resting', says the admonition over the door at **Wynand Fockink** (p36). The Dutch-gin maker's tasting room dates from 1679. The barkeep will pour your drink to the brim, so do like the locals to prevent spillage: lean over it and sip without lifting.

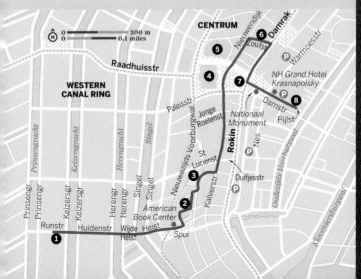

Best
Museums & Galleries

Amsterdam's world-class museums draw millions of visitors each year. The art collections take pride of place – you can't walk a kilometre here without bumping into a masterpiece. Canal-house museums are another local speciality. And, of course, the free-wheeling city has a fine assortment of oddball museums dedicated to everything from hash to houseboats.

☑ Top Tips

▶ Take advantage of e-tickets. Most sights sell them and there's little to no surcharge. They typically allow you to enter via a separate, faster queue.

▶ Queues are shortest during late afternoon and evening.

▶ Buy a discount card. In addition to saving on entrance fees, discount cards commonly provide fast-track entry.

All the Art

The Dutch Masters helped spawn the prolific art collections around town. You've probably heard of a few of these guys: Johannes Vermeer, Frans Hals and Rembrandt van Rijn. They came along during the Golden Age when a new, bourgeois society of merchants and shopkeepers were spending money to brighten up their homes and workplaces with fresh paintings. The masters were there to meet the need, and their output from the era now fills the city's top museums.

Other Treasures

The Netherlands' maritime prowess during the Golden Age also filled the coffers of local institutions. Silver, porcelain and colonial knick-knacks picked up on distant voyages form the basis of collections in the Rijksmuseum, Amsterdam Museum, Het Scheepvaartmuseum and Tropenmuseum.

Canal-House Museums

There are two kinds: the first preserves the house as a living space, with sumptuous interiors that show how the richest locals lived once upon a time, as at Museum Van Loon. The other type uses the elegant structure as a backdrop for unique collections, such as the Kattenkabinet for cat art.

Rijksmuseum (p86)

Best Art Museums

Van Gogh Museum
Hangs the world's largest collection of the tortured artist's vivid swirls. (p90)

Rijksmuseum The Netherlands' top treasure house bursts with Rembrandts, Vermeers, Delftware and more (p86)

Museum het Rembrandthuis Immerse yourself in the old master's paint-spattered studio and handsome home. (p128)

Stedelijk Museum Renowned modern art from Picasso to Mondrian to Warhol. (p97)

Hermitage Amsterdam The satellite of Russia's Hermitage Museum features one-off, blockbuster exhibits. (p72)

Foam Changing photography exhibits by world-renowned shutterbugs. (p72)

Best History Museums

Anne Frank Huis The Secret Annexe and Anne's claustrophobic bedroom serve as chilling reminders of WWII. (p44)

Amsterdam Museum Whiz-bang exhibits take you through the twists and turns of Amsterdam's convoluted history. (p30)

Verzetsmuseum Learn about WWII Dutch resistance fighters during the German occupation. (p135)

Worth a Trip

Designed by Dutch architect Wim Quist, the canalside **Cobra Museum** (www.cobra-museum.nl; Sandbergplein 1; adult/child €9.50/6; ⊙11am-5pm Tue-Sun; 🚊170, 172, 🚌5 Binnehof) is a light-flooded setting for works from the post-WWII CoBrA movement. The museum is full of their boldly coloured, avant-garde paintings, ceramics and statues, including many by Karel Appel, the style's most prolific practitioner.

Best
Parks & Gardens

Amsterdam has around 30 parks, so you're never far from a leafy refuge. City planners built in green spaces to provide relief from the densely packed neighbourhoods. They did a heck of a job. Enter the gates of Vondelpark or any of the other meadow-fringed landscapes, and you're hit with a potent shot of pastoral relaxation.

RACHEL LEWIS/GETTY IMAGES ©

Best for Strolling & Picnicking

Vondelpark Amsterdam's premier green scene is a mash-up of ponds, thickets and winding paths. (p94)

Westerpark Abutting a former gasworks building turned edgy cultural centre, the west side's rambling, reedy wilderness has become a hipster hang-out. (p65)

Sarphatipark De Pijp's lush oasis of rolling lawns, statues and fountains is similar to Vondelpark but without the crowds. (p107)

Oosterpark Political monuments and grey herons dot the sweeping expanse, built for nouveau-riche diamond traders a century ago. (p122)

Best Gardens

Hortus Botanicus When Dutch ships sailed afar in the 1600s, the tropical seeds they brought back were grown in this wonderful garden. (p136)

Begijnhof Push open the unassuming door and voila – a hidden courtyard of flowery gardens appears. (p26)

Rijksmuseum Big-name sculpture exhibitions pop up amid rose bushes and hedges in the museum's free, oft-overlooked gardens. (p86)

Museum Willet-Holthuysen A cosy French-style garden with sundial rolls out behind the gorgeous canal house. (p72)

☑ Top Tips

▸ Jan Pieter Heijestraat and Overtoom accommodate several delis and small markets that are handy for composing a picnic for Vondelpark.

▸ Delicious takeaway shops for picnic fixings line Haarlemmerstraat and Haarlemmerdijk leading into Westerpark.

▸ The Albert Cuypmarkt (p106) provides abundant supplies for outdoor meals in Sarphatipark.

Best
Canals

Amsterdammers have always known their Canal Ring, built during the Golden Age, is extraordinary. Unesco made it official in 2010, when it listed the waterways as a World Heritage site. Today the city has 165 canals spanned by 1753 bridges – more than any other city in the world.

LONELY PLANET/GETTY IMAGES ©

Best Views

Golden Bend Where the Golden Age magnates built their mansions along the regal Herengracht. (p69)

Reguliersgracht The tour favourite 'canal of seven bridges' is one of Amsterdam's most photographed vistas. (p82)

Prinsengracht The liveliest of Amsterdam's inner canals, with cafes, shops and houseboats lining the quays. (p59)

Brouwersgracht Among some seriously tough competition Amsterdammers swear this is the city's most beautiful canal. (p59)

Best Canal-Related Museums

Het Grachtenhuis Inventive multimedia displays explain how the Canal Ring and its

amazing houses were built. (p50)

Houseboat Museum Discover how *gezellig* (cosy) houseboat living can be aboard this 1914 sailing barge-turned-museum. (p51)

Best Canalside Dining

De Belhamel At the head of the Herengracht, this superb restaurant's tables along the canal are an aphrodisiac. (p53)

Buffet van Odette Simple, creative cooking overlooking the Prinsengracht's crooked canal houses. (p74)

Best Canalside Drinking

't Smalle Dock your boat right by the stone terrace of the 18th-century

☑ Top Tips

▶ If you'd like to cruise under your own steam, rent a boat from companies such as **Canal Motorboats** (📞020-422 70 07; www.canalmotorboats. com; Zandhoek 10a; rental 1st/2nd/3rd/4th hour €50/40/30/20, subsequent hours €20; 🕙10am-10pm; 🚊48 Barentszplein). A boat licence isn't required for boats under 15m in length or with a top speed of under 20km per hour.

former *jenever* (Dutch gin) distillery. (p55)

Hannekes Boom Local favourite with a gorgeous leafy beer garden on the water. (p138)

Best
Eating

Amsterdam's sizzling-hot foodie scene spans classic Dutch snacks to reinvented traditional recipes at contemporary restaurants, on-trend establishments pioneering world-first concepts, a wave of new ultra-healthy (often vegetarian or vegan) eateries, and an increasing focus on wine, cocktail and craft-beer pairings. And this multinational city has a cornucopia of cuisines from all over the globe.

Dutch Cuisine

Traditional Dutch cuisine revolves around meat, potatoes and vegetables. Typical dishes include *stamppot* (mashed pot) – potatoes mashed with another vegetable (usually kale or endive) and served with smoked sausage and strips of bacon.

Fresh winds are blowing through the Dutch traditional kitchen, breathing new life into centuries-old recipes by giving them a contemporary twist. Creative Dutch chefs are also taking concepts from the rest the world and melding them with locally sourced meats, seafood and vegetables.

New Trends

Concept restaurants are popping up all over the city, with kitchens often zeroing in on a single item, such as strawberries or avocados. Other current trends include gourmet street food (poké bowls, ramen, tacos, hot dogs...) as well as all-day brunch.

Foodhallen (p98), in the De Hallen tram depot-turned-cultural complex, has a host of eateries under one roof, and is a fantastic place to take the city's dining temperature.

LONELY PLANET/GETTY IMAGES ©

☑ **Top Tips**

▶ Phone ahead to make a reservation for eateries in the middle and upper price brackets. Nearly everyone speaks English. Many places offer online booking options.

▶ Many restaurants, even top-end ones, don't accept credit cards. Or if they do, there's often a 5% surcharge. Conversely, some places accept cards only. Check first.

Traditional Dutch pea soup

Best Dutch

Lt Cornelis Cutting-edge Dutch cooking and craft cocktails. (p34)

Greetje Resurrects Dutch classics, with mouthwatering results. (p136)

D'Vijff Vlieghen A treasure rambling through five 17th-century canal houses. (p33)

Ron Gastrobar Dutch-style tapas from the city's top chef. (p99)

Best Indonesian

Dèsa Hugely popular for its *rijsttafel* (rice table) banquets. (p112)

Blue Pepper Gourmet Indonesian cuisine. (p100)

Best Surinamese

Tokoman Hot-spiced Surinamese sandwiches. (p138)

Roopram Roti No-frills spot for flaky roti and fiery hot sauce. (p124)

Best Budget

Avocado Show Avocados feature in everything from salad bowls to ice cream and cocktails. (p110)

Butcher Huge, fresh burgers made right in front of you. (p111)

Vleminckx Amsterdam's best *frites* (fries). (p33)

Best for Foodies

Gartine Slow-food sandwiches and a dazzling high tea hide in the city centre. (p33)

De Kas Dine in the greenhouse that grew your meal's ingredients. (p122)

Graham's Kitchen Ingredients at this diamond find are sourced from the Amsterdam area. (p112)

Best Brunch

Bakers & Roasters Banana nutbread French toast and Bloody Marys at Amsterdam's brunch specialist. (p110)

Scandinavian Embassy Goat's-milk yoghurt, salmon on Danish rye bread and more dishes from northern lands. (p111)

Best
Drinking & Nightlife

Amsterdam is one of the wildest nightlife cities in Europe and the world. Beyond the Red Light District and hot spots around Leidseplein and Rembrandtplein, the clubbing scene is also rapidly expanding thanks to 24-hour-licensed venues. Yet you can easily avoid a hardcore party scene: Amsterdam remains a *café* (pub) society where the pursuit of pleasure centres on cosiness and charm.

Brown Cafes

Amsterdam is famed for its historic *bruin cafés* (traditional Dutch pubs). The name comes from the nicotine stains from centuries of use (although recent aspirants slap on brown paint to catch up). Occasionally you'll find sand on the wooden floor to soak up spilt beer. Most importantly, the city's *bruin cafés* provide an atmosphere conducive to conversation – and the nirvana of *gezelligheid* (conviviality, cosiness).

Clubbing

Amsterdam is banging on Berlin's door to claim the mantle of Europe's clubbing capital. The electronic music extravaganza **Amsterdam Dance Event** (ADE; https://amsterdam-dance-event.nl; ⏰late Oct) is a fixture on the city's calendar, and in 2012 nightclub promoter Mirik Milan became Amsterdam's (and the world's) inaugural *nachtburgemeester* (night mayor), representing and encouraging the city's nightlife and economy.

Inner-city clubs are integrating into the social fabric, and epic venues (including some with new 24-hour licences) are opening in repurposed buildings outside the city centre to avoid noise, and are reachable by public transport. In addition to club nights, they mount multi-genre art exhibitions, markets and other diverse cultural offerings.

☑ Top Tips

▶ *Café* means pub; a coffeeshop is where one gets marijuana.

▶ *Een bier*, *een pils* or *een vaasje* is a normal-sized glass of beer; *een kleintje pils* is a small glass.

▶ A *koffie* is black; *koffie verkeerd* (coffee 'wrong') is made with milk, similar to a caffe latte.

't Smalle (p55)

Best Brown Cafes

In 't Aepjen Candles burn all day long in the time-warped, 500-year-old house. (p35)

Hoppe An icon of drinking history. (p37)

De Sluyswacht Swig in the lock-keeper's quarters across from Rembrandt's house. (p140)

Best Tasting Houses

Wynand Fockink The 1679 tasting house pours glorious *jenevers*. (p36)

In de Olofspoort Stocks stocks over 200 varieties. (p36)

Best Beer

Brouwerij 't IJ Wonderful independent brewery at the foot of the De Gooyer windmill. (p138)

Oedipus Brewery & Tap Room Brilliant brewery in Amsterdam Noord. (p148)

Best Cocktail Bars

Tales & Spirits House infusions and vintage glasses. (p35)

Dum Dum Palace Classic cocktails with Asian twists. (p36)

Best Coffeeshops

Dampkring Hollywood made the hobbit-like decor and prize-winning product famous. (p34)

Abraxas A haven of mellow music and comfy sofas spread over three floors. (p34)

Worth a Trip

In an industrial estate at Sloter-dijk, **Warehouse Elementenstraat** (www.elementenstraat.nl; Elementenstraat 25; ⏰ hours vary; 🛜; 🚌 748 Contactweg, Ⓜ Isolatorweg) has four enormous halls with phenomenal lighting and sound systems that accommodate up to 2500 clubbers, who come to dance to house, techno and other EDM styles 24 hours. Check ahead as events often sell out. Door tickets are cash only.

Best
Shopping

During the Golden Age, Amsterdam was the world's warehouse, stuffed with riches from the far corners of the earth. The capital's cupboards are still stocked with all kinds of exotica (just look at that Red Light gear!), but the real pleasure here is finding some odd, tiny shop selling something you wouldn't find anywhere else.

Specialities & Souvenirs

Dutch fashion is all about cool, practical designs that don't get caught in bike spokes. Dutch-designed homewares bring a stylish touch to everyday objects. Antiques, art and vintage goodies also rank high on the local list. Popular gifts include tulip bulbs, Gouda cheese and bottles of *jenever* (Dutch gin). Blue-and-white Delft pottery is a widely available quality souvenir. And, of course, clogs, bongs and pot-leaf-logo T-shirts are in great supply

Shopping Streets

The busiest shopping streets are Kalverstraat by the Dam and Leidsestraat, which leads into Leidseplein. Both are lined with department stores, such as Dutch retailers Hema and De Bijenkorf. The Old South's PC Hooftstraat lines up Chanel, Diesel, Gucci and other fancy fashion brands along its length.

Boutiques & Antiques

At the top of the Jordaan, Haarlemmerstraat and Haarlemmerdijk are lined with hip boutiques and food shops. Just to the south, the Negen Straatjes (Nine Streets) offers a satisfying browse among offbeat, pint-sized shops. Antique and art buffs should head for the Southern Canal Ring's Spiegel Quarter, along Spiegelgracht and Nieuwe Spiegelstraat.

MATTEO ZAABO/CHEST OF DRAWERS FOR DROOG BY TEJO REMY ©

☑ **Top Tips**

▸ Department stores and large shops generally open seven days; some smaller shops close on Sunday and/or Monday.

▸ Many shops stay open late (to 9pm) Thursday.

▸ Useful words to know: *kassa* (cashier), *korting* (discount) and *uitverkoop* (clearance sale).

Mushrooms at Noordermarkt (p47)

Best Markets

Albert Cuypmarkt
Vibrant street market spilling over with food, fashion and bargain finds. (p106)

Waterlooplein Flea Market Piles of curios for treasure hunters. (p131)

Noordermarkt It's morning bliss trawling for organic foods and vintage clothes. (p47)

Best Dutch Design

Droog The famed collective is known for sly, playful, repurposed and reinvented homewares. (p141)

Frozen Fountain Amsterdam's best-known showcase of Dutch-designed furniture and homewares. (p60)

Hutspot Funky store giving emerging designers an opportunity to sell their work. (p114)

Mobilia Dutch design is stunningly showcased at this three-storey 'lifestyle studio'. (p83)

X Bank Dazzling displays change monthly. (p40)

Best Fashion

Young Designers United Tomorrow's big names jam the racks here. (p82)

By AMFI Students and alumni of the Amsterdam Fashion Institute sell their wares. (p40)

VLVT Up-and-coming Dutch-designed women's fashion on chic Cornelis Schuytstraat. (p103)

Good Genes De Pijp-designed jeans. (p115)

Best Souvenirs

Bloemenmarkt Bulbs, bulbs and more bulbs fill Amsterdam's 'floating' flower market. (p68)

Galleria d'Arte Rinascimento Royal Delftware ceramics (both antique and new). (p62)

Mark Raven Grafiek Artsy, beyond-the-norm T-shirts and prints of the city. (p40)

Museum Shop at the Museumplein The one-stop shop for all your Rembrandt, Vermeer and Van Gogh items. (p103)

Best
For Free

Although the costs of Amsterdam's accommodation and dining can mount up, there's a bright side. Not only is the entire Canal Ring a Unesco World Heritage Site (effectively a free living museum), but almost every day you'll find things to do and see that are free (or virtually free).

NATTEE CHALERMTIRAGOOL/SHUTTERSTOCK ©

Free Sights

Civic Guard Gallery Stroll through the monumental collection of portraits, from Golden Age to modern. (p32)

Rijksmuseum Gardens These Renaissance and baroque gardens, with rose bushes, hedges and statues, are free to enter. (p86)

Begijnhof Explore the 14th-century hidden courtyard and its clandestine churches. (p26)

Stadsarchief You never know what treasures you'll find in the vaults of the city's archives. (p73)

Gassan Diamonds Distinguish your princess from marquise, river from top cape. (p136)

ARCAM A fascinating look at Amsterdam's architecture – past, present and future. (p136)

Kunststad (Art City) Wander through these vast artist studios in Amsterdam Noord. (p146)

NEMO roof terrace One of the best views of Amsterdam extends from the roof of this landmark building. (p134)

Free Entertainment

Concertgebouw Hosts free lunchtime concerts on Wednesday (September to June). (p102)

Muziektheater Free classical concerts during lunch most Tuesdays (September to May). (p139)

Bimhuis Jazz sessions hot up the revered venue on Tuesday nights. (p140)

Openluchttheater Vondelpark's outdoor theatre

 Top Tips

▶ Visit www.wifi-amsterdam.nl to find free hot spots around town.

▶ Yellow Backie (www.yellowbackie.org) lets visitors catch a free ride on the back of a local's bike. When you see someone cycling by with a bright-yellow luggage rack on the rear, yell 'Backie!' The rider will stop, let you hop on, and pedal you onward.

puts on concerts and kids' shows throughout summer. (p103)

EYE Film Institute Has pods in the basement where you can watch free films. (p146)

Best
For Kids

KAVALENKAV/SHUTTERSTOCK ©

Breathe easy: you've landed in one of Europe's most kid-friendly cities. The small scale, the quirky buildings, the lack of car traffic and the canals all combine to make it a wondrous place for little ones. And the Dutch seem to always be dreaming up creative ways to entertain youngsters.

Best Thrills

NEMO Kid-focused, hands-on science labs inside and a terrace with a splashy summer water feature outside. (p134)

Het Scheepvaartmuseum Climb aboard the full-scale, 17th-century replica ship and check out the cannons. (p134)

Tropenmuseum Spend the afternoon learning to yodel, sitting in a yurt or travelling via otherworldly exhibits. (p118)

Vondelpark Space-age slides at the western end, playground in the middle, duck ponds throughout. (p94)

Artis Royal Zoo Extrovert monkeys, big cats, shimmying fish and a planetarium provide all the requisite thrills. (p134)

Centrale Bibliotheek Amsterdam Has a whole children's floor with storytimes, reading lounges and books in English. (p135)

Micropia The world's first microbe museum has a wall of poop, a kissing meter and other inventive exhibits. (p134)

Best Kids' Shops

Het Oud-Hollandsch Snoepwinkeltje Stocks jar after jar of Dutch penny sweets. (p61)

Knuffels Cuddly stuffed animals, spinning mobiles, puppets and puzzles will please young ones. (p141)

Mechanisch Speelgoed Nostalgic wind-up toys. (p62)

☑ Top Tips

▶ For admission prices 'child' is usually defined as under 18 years. But at many tourist sites, the cut-off age for free or reduced rates is 12. Some sights may only provide free entry to children under six.

▶ Most bike rental shops rent bikes with baby or child seats.

▶ Many higherend hotels arrange babysitting services for a fee.

Best
Entertainment

Amsterdam supports a flourishing arts scene, with loads of big concert halls, theatres, cinemas, comedy clubs and other performance venues filled on a regular basis. Music fans are superbly catered for here, and there is a fervent subculture for just about every genre, especially jazz, classical, rock and avant-garde beats.

INGOLF POMPE / LOOK-FOTO/GETTY IMAGES ©

Music

Live music in all genres regularly plays at venues throughout the city.

Jazz is extremely popular, from far-out, improvisational stylings to more traditional notes. The grand Bimhuis (p140) is the big game in town. Smaller jazz venues abound and it's easy to find a live combo.

Amsterdam's classical-music scene, with top international orchestras, conductors and soloists crowding the agenda, is the envy of many European cities. Choose between the flawless Concertgebouw or dramatic Muziekgebouw aan 't IJ for the main shows.

Many of the city's nightclubs also host live rock bands. Huge touring names often play smallish venues such as the Melkweg and Paradiso; it's a real treat to catch one of your favourites here.

Comedy & Theatre

Given that the Dutch are fine linguists with a keen sense of humour, English-language comedy thrives in Amsterdam, especially around the Jordaan. Local theatre tends toward the edgy and experimental.

Cinema

Amsterdam is a cinephile's favourite, with oodles of art-house cinemas.

☑ Top Tips

▶ The **Last Minute Ticket Shop** (www. lastminuteticketshop. nl; ⏱online ticket sales from 10am on day of performance; 🚊1/2/5/7/10 Leidseplein) sells same-day half-price tickets for concerts, performances and even club nights online. Events are handily marked 'LNP' (language no problem) if understanding Dutch isn't vital.

▶ I Amsterdam (www.iamsterdam. com) has events listings. Check Film Ladder (www.filmladder. nl/amsterdam) for movie listings.

ANGELO CAVALLI/GETTY IMAGES ©

Muziekgebouw aan 't IJ and Bimhuis (p140)

Best Rock

Melkweg Housed in a former dairy, it's Amsterdam's coolest club-gallery-cinema-concert hall. (p81)

Paradiso One-time church that preaches a gospel of rock. (p81)

OCCII A former squat that gives the night to edgy alternative bands. (p95)

De Nieuwe Anita Rock out by the stage behind the bookcase-concealed door. (p58)

Best Classical & Opera

Muziekgebouw aan 't IJ Stunning high-tech temple of the performing arts. (p140)

Concertgebouw World-renowned concert hall with superb acoustics. (p102)

Conservatorium van Amsterdam See recitals by students at Amsterdam's snazzy conservatory of music. (p140)

Best Comedy & Theatre

Boom Chicago Laugh-out-loud improv-style comedy in the Jordaan. (p58)

Stadsschouwburg Large-scale plays, operettas and festivals right on Leidseplein. (p69)

Best Cinemas

EYE Film Institute New, old, foreign, domestic: the Netherlands' uber-mod film centre shows quality films of all kinds. (p146)

Pathé Tuschinskitheater Amsterdam's most famous cinema, with a sumptuous art-deco/Amsterdam School interior. (p80)

Movies Amsterdam's oldest cinema dates from 1912. (p60)

Best
Gay & Lesbian

To call Amsterdam a gay capital doesn't express just how welcoming and open the scene is here. The Netherlands was the first country to legalise same-sex marriage (in 2001), so it's no surprise that Amsterdam's gay scene is among the world's largest.

AN JO KAN/SHUTTERSTOCK ©

Party Zones

Five hubs party hardest. **Warmoesstraat** in the Red Light District hosts the infamous, kink-filled leather and fetish bars. Nearby on the upper end of the **Zeedijk** crowds spill onto laid-back bar terraces (though some long-time favourites have closed recently).

In the Southern Canal Ring, the area around **Rembrandtplein** (aka the 'Amstel area') has traditional pubs and *bruin cafés,* some with a campy bent. **Leidseplein** has a smattering of high-action clubs along Kerkstraat.

And **Reguliersdwarsstraat**, located one street down from the flower market, draws the beautiful crowd at its trendy, fickle hot spots.

Best Gay & Lesbian Hangouts

't Mandje Amsterdam's oldest gay bar is a trinket-covered beauty. (p37)

Montmartre Legendary bar where Dutch ballads and old top-40 hits tear the roof off. (p80)

De Trut A Sunday fixture on the scene. (p58)

Taboo Bar Drag shows and party games. (p79)

☑ Top Tips

▶ Gay Amsterdam (www.gayamster dam. com) lists hotels, shops and clubs, and provides maps.

▶ Information kiosk/ souvenir shop **Pink Point** (☎020-428 1070; www.facebook. com/pinkpointamster dam; Westermarkt; ⊙10.30am-6pm; 🚋13/14/17 Westermarkt) has details of parties, events and social groups.

▶ **Amsterdam Gay Pride** (https://pride. amsterdam; ⊙late Jul–early Aug) features the world's only waterborne Pride parade.

Best Tours

Best Walking Tours

Sandeman's New Amsterdam Tours (www.neweuropetours.eu; by donation; ☺up tu 8 tours daily; 🚊4/9/16/24 Dam) Energetic young guides working on a tip-only basis lead a 2½-hour jaunt past the city centre's top sights.

Hungry Birds Street Food Tours (📞06 1898 6268; www.hungrybirds.nl; day/night tour per person €79/89; ☺Mon-Sat) Guides take you 'off the eaten track' to visit around 10 spots over four hours. Prices include food.

Mee in Mokum (www.gildeamsterdam.nl; Gedempte Begijnensloot; tours adult/child €7.50/5; ☺11am & 2pm Tue-Sun; 🚊1/2/5 Spui) Low-priced walkabouts lasting two to three hours, led by volunteers. Reserve at least a day ahead and pay cash on the day.

Best Bicycle Tours

Mike's Bike Tours (📞020-622 79 70; www.

mikesbiketoursamsterdam.com; Prins Hendrikkade 176a; city tours per adult/13-18yr from €28/25, countryside from €32; ☺office 9am-6pm Mar-Oct, from 10am Nov-Feb; 🚊16/24 Keizersgracht) Offers city, countryside and harbour tours.

Yellow Bike (📞020-620 69 40; www.yellowbike.nl; Nieuwezijds Kolk 29; city tours from €23.50, Waterland tour €33.50; ☺Mar-Oct; 🚊1/2/5/13/17 Nieuwezijds Kolk) City tours and a longer countryside tour.

Best Boat Tours

Those Dam Boat Guys (📞06 1885 5219; www.thosedamboatguys.com; tours €25; ☺11am, 1pm, 3pm, 5pm & 7pm Mar-Sep; 🚊13/14/17 Westermarkt) Cheeky small tours (maximum 10 people) on electric boats. Feel free to bring food, beer, smoking material and whatever else you want for the 90-minute jaunt.

Blue Boat Company (📞02 0679 1370; www.blueboat.nl; Stadhouderskade 30; 75min tour adult/child €17/8.50; ☺half-hourly tour 10am-6pm Mar-Oct, hourly Nov-Feb; 🚊1/2/5/7/10 Leidseplein) The 75-minute main tour glides by the top sights. Ninety-minute evening cruises (adult/child €19.50/15.50) are offered at 8pm.

Rederji Lampedusa (www.rederjilampedusa.nl; canal tour 1-2hr €17, VIP tours by donation; ☺canal tours Sat & Sun, VIP tours Fri fortnightly May-Sep; 🚊26 Muziekgebouw) Take a canal-boat tour or a sunset trip around Amsterdam harbour aboard former refugee boats, with commentary on the history of immigration.

Best
Cycling

Bicycles are more common than cars in Amsterdam, and to roll like a local you'll need a two-wheeler. Rent one from the myriad outlets around town or your accommodation, and the whole city becomes your playground. Cycling is *the* quintessential activity while visiting.

BURCIN TUNCER/GETTY IMAGES ©

Journey Planning

Online journey planners include Fietsersbond (https://routeplanner .fietsersbond.nl), Holland Cycling (www. holland-cycling.com), Routecraft (www.route craft.com/fietsroute planner-amsterdam. html) and Route You (www.routeyou.com), which is good for scenic routes.

Road Rules

Helmets aren't compulsory. Most Dutch cyclists don't use them and they don't come standard with rental.

Amsterdam has 500km of bike paths. Use the bicycle lane on the road's right-hand side, marked by white lines and bike symbols. Cycling on footpaths is illegal.

Cycle in the same direction as traffic and adhere to all traffic lights and signs. Hand signal when turning.

A bell is mandatory; ring it as often as necessary.

After dark, a white or yellow headlight and red tail light are required by law.

Park only in bicycle racks near train and tram stations and in certain public squares (or risk the removal of your bike by the police).

Best Cycling Spots

Vondelpark Urban oasis. (p94)

Eastern Islands Contemporary architecture. (p126)

Amsterdam Noord Windmills and farmland. (p142)

☑ Top Tips

▶ Most bikes come with two locks: one for the front wheel (attach it to the bike frame), the other for the back. One of these locks should also be attached to a fixed structure (preferably a bike rack).

▶ Cross tram rails at a sharp angle to avoid getting stuck.

▶ If your bike goes missing, call the Fietsdepot (Bike Depository) at ☎020-334 45 22 to see if it was removed by the city (perhaps for being parked in an unsafe spot). If not, call the police on ☎0900 88 44 or visit the local station to report it as stolen.

Survival Guide

Survival Guide

Before You Go

When to Go

Amsterdam

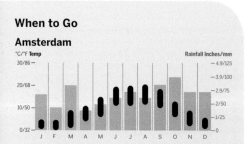

→ **Spring (Mar–May)**
Tulip time! Crowds amass around King's Day (27 April). Alternating rainy and gorgeous weather.

→ **Summer (Jun–Aug)**
Peak season, warm with lots of daylight, cafe terraces boom, festivals aplenty.

→ **Autumn (Sep–Nov)**
Can be rainy, off-peak rates return, the regular cultural season starts up.

→ **Winter (Dec–Feb)**
Ice-skating fun, cosy cafes with fireplaces, and low-season rates ease the dark, chilly days.

Book Your Stay

→ Book as far in advance as possible, especially for festival, summer and weekend visits.

→ Many hotels offer discounts if you book directly via their websites.

→ City hotel tax is due to rise to at least 6% in 2018.

→ If you're paying by credit card, some hotels add a surcharge of up to 5%.

Useful Websites

Lonely Planet (www.lonely planet.com/amsterdam/ hotels) Recommendations and bookings.

I Amsterdam (www.iam sterdam.com) Wide range of options from the city's official website.

Hotels.nl (www.hotels. nl) For deals on larger properties.

CityMundo (https://am sterdam.citymundo. com) Reliable broker for apartment and houseboat rentals.

Best Budget

Cocomama (☏020-627 24 54; www.cocomamahostel. com; Westeinde 18; d €107-212, 4/6-bed dm €44/39, min 2 night stay; @☏; 🚊4/25 Stadhouderskade) Red-curtained boutique hostel in a former brothel.

Generator Amsterdam (☏020-708 56 00; www. generatorhostels.com; Mauritskade 57; dm €40, d €70-170, q €160-360; ☏; 🚊9/10/14 Alexanderplein) Posh new hostel with bars overlooking Oosterpark.

Stayokay Amsterdam Stadsdoelen (☏020-624 68 32; www.stayokay.com; Kloveniersburgwal 97; dm €32.50-51, tw/d from €90-150; @☏; 🚊4/9/14/16/24 Muntplein) Bustling backpacker digs near Nieuwmarkt square.

Best Midrange

Hotel Fita (☏020-679 09 76; www.fita.nl; Jan Luijkenstraat 37; s/d from €120/140; ☏; 🚊2/3/5/12 Van Baerlestraat) Sweet little family-owned hotel a stone's throw from the Museumplein.

Hotel V (☏020-662 32 33; www.hotelvfrederikplein. nl; Weteringschans 136; d

€93-154; ☏; 🚊4/7/10 Frederiksplein) A retro-chic hotel facing lush Frederiksplein.

Conscious Hotel Vondelpark (☏020-820 33 33; www.conscioushotels. com; Overtoom 519; d/tr from €90/121.50; ☏; 🚊1 Rhijnvis Feithstraat) Eco innovations include recycled materials and a living wall.

Best Top End

Hotel Okura Amsterdam (☏020-678 71 11; www. okura.nl; Ferdinand Bolstraat 333; d/ste from €270/355; ❄@☏✉; 🚊12 Cornelis Troostplein) Rare-for-Amsterdam views and four Michelin stars in the building.

Toren (☏020-622 63 52; www.thetoren.nl; Keizersgracht 164; s/d/tr/ste from €108/189/225/342; ❄@☏; 🚊13/14/17 Westermarkt) Blends 17th-century opulence with a sensual decadence.

College Hotel (☏020-571 15 11; www.thecollegehotel. com; Roelof Hartstraat 1; d from €169; ❄☏; 🚊3/5/12/24 Roelof Hartplein) Impeccably run by hotel-school students

Arriving in Amsterdam

Schiphol International Airport (AMS)

Train Trains run to Amsterdam's Centraal Station (€5.20 one way, 15 minutes) 24 hours a day. From 6am to 12.30am they go every 10 minutes or so; hourly in the wee hours. The rail platform is inside the terminal, down the escalator.

Shuttle bus A shuttle van is run by **Connexxion** (www.schipholhotelshuttle. nl; one way/return €17/27), every 30 minutes from 7am to 9pm, from the airport for several hotels. Look for the Connexxion desk by Arrivals 4.

Bus Bus 197/Amsterdam Airport Express (€5 one way, 25 minutes) is the quickest way to places by the Museumplein, Leidseplein or Vondelpark. It departs outside the arrivals hall door. Buy a ticket from the driver.

Taxi Taxis take 20 to 30 minutes to the centre (longer in heavy traffic), costing around €37.50. The taxi stand is just outside the arrivals hall door.

Centraal Train Station

Tram Of Amsterdam's 15 tram lines, 10 stop at Centraal Station, and then fan out to the rest of the city. For trams 4, 9, 16, 24 and 26, head far to the left (east) when you come out the station's main entrance; look for the 'A' sign. For trams 1, 2, 5, 13 and 17, head to the right (west) and look for the 'B' sign.

Taxi Taxis queue near the front station entrance toward the west side. Fares are meter-based. It should be €15 to €20 for destinations in the centre, canal ring or Jordaan.

Journey Planner

Website 9292 (https://9292.nl) calculates routes, costs and travel times, and will get you from door to door, wherever you're going in the city. The site is in English and Dutch.

Getting Around

Tram

➡ Most public transport within the city is by tram. The vehicles are fast, frequent and ubiquitous, operating between 6am and 12.30am.

➡ Tickets are not sold on board. Buy a disposable OV-chipkaart (www.ov-chipkaart.nl; one hour €2.90) or a day pass from the GVB information office, located across the tram tracks from Centraal Station, attached to the VVV I Amsterdam Visitor Centre.

➡ When you enter *and* exit, wave your card at the pink machine to 'check in' and 'check out'.

➡ Most tram lines start at Centraal Station and then fan out into the neighbourhoods.

Metro & Bus

➡ Amsterdam's buses and metro (subway) primarily serve outer districts. Prices for the metro and most buses are the same as trams.

➡ *Nachtbussen* (night buses) run after other

transport stops (from 1am to 6am, every hour). A ticket costs €4.50.

Bicycle

➡ Rental shops are everywhere.

➡ You'll have to show a passport or European national ID card and leave a credit-card imprint or pay a deposit (usually €50 to €100).

➡ Prices per 24-hour period for basic 'coaster-brake' bikes average €12. Bikes with gears and handbrakes cost more.

➡ Theft insurance costs around €3 to €5 extra per day and is strongly advised.

➡ **Ajax Bike** (☑06 1729 4284; www.ajaxbike.nl; Gerard Doustraat 153; bike rental per 4/24hr from €6.50/9; ⏰10am-5.30pm Mon-Sat, noon-4pm Sun; 🚋4 Stadhouderskade) is in De Pijp.

➡ **Bike City** (☑020-626 37 21; https://bikecity.nl; Bloemgracht 68-70; bike rental per day from €14; ⏰9am-5.30pm; 🚋13/14/17 Westermarkt) is in Jordaan.

➡ **Black Bikes** (☑0852 737 454; http://black-bikes.com; Nieuwezijds Voorburgwal 146; bike rental per 3/24hr from €9/13, electric bikes

€24/37.50; ⏰8am-8pm
Mon-Fri, 9am-7pm Sat & Sun;
🚇1/2/5/13/14/17 Raad-
huisstraat) has 10 shops,
including this one in the
centre.

➡ **Damstraat Rent-a-
Bike** (📞020-625 50 29;
www.rentabike.nl; Damstraat
20-22; bike rental per 3/24hr
from €7/9.25; ⏰9am-6pm;
🚇4/9/16/24 Dam) is near
the Dam.

➡ **MacBike** (📞020-620
09 85; www.macbike.nl;
De Ruijterkade 34b; bike
rental per 3/24hr from
€11/14.75; ⏰9am-5.45pm;
🚇1/2/4/5/9/13/16/17/24
Centraal Station) has a
convenient location at
Centraal Station, plus
others at Waterlooplein
and Leidseplein.

➡ Alternatively, locate
bikes around town via
the app FlickBike (www.
flickbike.nl); rental per 30
minutes costs €1. Scan
the QR code to unlock/
lock the bike. It can be returned to any Amsterdam
bike rack.

Taxi

➡ Taxis are expensive and
not very speedy given
Amsterdam's maze of
streets.

➡ You don't hail taxis on
the road. Instead, find

Tickets & Passes

➡ The GVB offers unlimited-ride passes for one
to seven days (€7.50 to €34), valid on trams,
some buses and the metro.

➡ Passes are available at the **GVB information
office** (www.gvb.nl; Stationsplein 10; ⏰7am-9pm
Mon-Fri, 8am-9pm Sat & Sun; 🚇1/2/4/5/9/13/16/17/24
Centraal Station) and **VVV I Amsterdam Visitor Centres** (Map p28; 📞020-702 60 00; www.
iamsterdam.com, Stationsplein 10; ⏰9am-5pm Mon-Sat;
🚇1/2/4/5/9/13/16/17/24 Centraal Station), but not
onboard.

➡ The I Amsterdam Card (www.iamsterdam.com;
per 24/48/72/96 hours €57/67/77/87) includes
a GVB travel pass in its fee.

➡ The Amsterdam Travel Ticket (per one/two/
three days €16/21/26) is a GVB unlimited-ride
pass with an airport train ticket added on. Buy it
at the airport (at the NS ticket window) or GVB
office.

them at stands at Cen-
traal Station, Leidseplein
and other busy spots
around town. You needn't
take the first car in the
queue.

➡ Another method is to
book a taxi by phone.
Taxicentrale Amsterdam
(TCA; 📞020-777 77 77; www.
tcataxi.nl) is the most reliable company.

➡ Fares are meter-based.
The meter starts at
€2.95, then it's €2.17 per
kilometre thereafter. A
ride from Leidseplein to
the Dam costs about €12;

from Centraal Station to
Jordaan is €10 to €15.

Car

➡ Parking is expensive
and scarce.

➡ Street parking in the
centre costs around
€5/30 per hour/day. Pay
online at www.3377.nl.

➡ It's better (and
cheaper) to leave your
vehicle in a park-and-ride
lot at the edge of town.
See www.iamsterdam.
com for details.

➡ All the big multinational rental companies are in town; many have offices on Overtoom, near the Vondelpark.

Train

➡ Trains run by NS (www. ns.nl) serve the outer suburbs and, aside from travelling to/from the airport, most visitors will rarely need to use them unless undertaking day trips further afield.

➡ Tickets can be bought at the NS service desk windows or at ticketing machines.

➡ Pay with cash, debit or credit card. Visa and MasterCard are accepted, though there is a €0.50 surcharge to use them, and they must have chip-and-PIN technology.

➡ If you want to use a ticketing machine and pay cash, know that they accept coins only (no paper bills). The machines have instructions in English.

➡ Check in *and* out with your ticket/card. Tap it against the card reader in the gates or free-standing posts. You'll hear one beep to enter, and two beeps when departing.

Essential Information

Business Hours

Opening hours often decrease during off-peak months (October to Easter).

Cafés (pubs), bars and coffeeshops Open noon (exact hours vary); most close 1am Sunday to Thursday, 3am Friday and Saturday

General office hours 8.30am to 5pm Monday to Friday

Museums 10am to 5pm, though some close Monday

Restaurants 11am to 2.30pm and 6pm to 10pm

Shops 9am/10am to 6pm Monday to Saturday, noon to 6pm Sunday. Smaller shops may keep shorter hours and/or close Monday. Many shops stay open late (to 9pm) Thursday.

Supermarkets 8am to 8pm; in the city centre some stay open until 9pm or 10pm

Discount Cards

I Amsterdam Card (www.iamsterdam.com; per 24/48/72/96 hours €57/67/77/87) provides admission to more than 30 museums (though not the Rijksmuseum), a canal cruise, and discounts at shops, entertainment venues and restaurants. Also includes a GVB transit pass. Useful for quick visits to the city. Available at VVV I Amsterdam Visitor Centres and some hotels.

Electricity

Type C
220V/50Hz

**Type F
230V/50Hz**

Money-saving Tips

➡ Free sights and entertainment are plentiful (see p166).

➡ Order the *dagschotel* (dish of the day) or *dagmenu* (set menu of three or more courses) at restaurants.

➡ Check the Last Minute Ticket Shop (www. lastminuteticketshop.nl) for half-price, same-day seats for all kinds of performances.

Money

A surprising number of businesses do not accept credit cards, so it's wise to have cash on hand. Conversely, many places only accept cards.

ATMs

➡ Most ATMs accept credit cards such as Visa and MasterCard, as well as cash cards that access the Cirrus and Plus networks.

➡ ATMs are not hard to find, but in the city centre and at the airport, they often have queues or run out of cash on weekends.

Changing Money

➡ GWK Travelex has several branches around town including **Centraal Station** (📞020-627 27 31; www.gwktravelex.nl; Stationsplein; 🕓8am-8pm Mon-Sat, 10am-5pm Sun), Leidseplein and Schiphol Airport.

Credit Cards

➡ Most hotels and large stores accept major international credit cards.

➡ Many shops, restaurants and other businesses (including supermarket chain Albert Heijn) do not accept credit cards, or only accept debit cards with chip-and-PIN technology.

➡ Be aware that foreign-issued cards (even chip-and-PIN-enabled foreign credit or debit cards) aren't always accepted, so ask first.

➡ Some establishments levy a 5% surcharge (or more) on credit cards to offset the commissions charged by card providers. Always check first.

Tipping

Bars Not expected.

Hotels €1 to €2 per bag for porters; not typical for cleaning staff.

Restaurants Leave 5% to 10% for a cafe snack (if your bill comes to €9.50, you might round up to €10), 10% or so for a restaurant meal.

Taxis Tip 5% to 10%, or round up to the nearest euro.

Public Holidays

Most museums adopt Sunday hours on public holidays (except Christmas and New Year, when they close), even if they fall on a day when the place would otherwise be closed, such as Monday.

Nieuwjaarsdag (New Year's Day) 1 January

Goede Vrijdag (Good Friday) March/April

Eerste Paasdag (Easter Sunday) March/April

Tweede Paasdag (Easter Monday) March/April

Koningsdag (King's Day) 27 April

Dodenherdenking (Remembrance Day) 4 May (unofficial)

Bevrijdingsdag (Liberation Day) 5 May (unofficially celebrated annually; officially every five years, next in 2020)

Hemelvaartsdag (Ascension Day) 40th day after Easter Sunday

Eerste Pinksterdag (Whit Sunday; Pentecost) 50th day after Easter Sunday

Tweede Pinksterdag (Whit Monday) 50th day after Easter Monday

Eerste Kerstdag (Christmas Day) 25 December

Tweede Kerstdag (Second Christmas; Boxing Day) 26 December

Safe Travel

Amsterdam is a safe and manageable city and if you use your common sense you should have no problems.

➜ Be alert for pickpockets in tourist-heavy zones such as Centraal Station, the Bloemenmarkt and Red Light District.

➜ Avoid deserted streets in the Red Light District at night.

➜ It is forbidden to take photos of women in the Red Light District windows; this is strictly enforced.

➜ Be careful around the canals. Almost none of them have fences or barriers.

➜ Watch out for bicycles; never walk in bicycle lanes and always look carefully before you cross one.

Telephone

Mobile Phones

➜ Ask your home provider about an international plan.

➜ Alternatively, local prepaid SIM cards are widely available and can be used in most unlocked phones.

➜ The EU has abolished international roaming costs, but beware of high roaming charges from other countries.

Telephone Codes

➜ Drop the leading 0 on numbers if you're calling from outside the Netherlands.

➜ To call internationally from within the Netherlands, first dial the exit code ☎00.

➜ **Netherlands country code** ☎31

➜ **Amsterdam city code** ☎020

➜ **Free calls** ☎0800

➜ **Mobile numbers** ☎06

➜ **Paid information calls** ☎0900, cost varies

Toilets

➜ Public toilets are not a widespread facility on Dutch streets, apart from the free-standing public urinals for men in places such as the Red Light District.

➡ Many people duck into a *café* (pub) or department store.

➡ The standard fee for toilet attendants is €0.50.

➡ The app HogeNood (High Need; www. hogenood.nu) maps the nearest toilets based on your location.

Tourist Information

I Amsterdam Visitor Centre (Map p28; ☏020-702 60 00; www.iamsterdam. com; Stationsplein 10; ◷9am-5pm Mon-Sat; ◻1/2/4/5/9/13/16/17/24 Centraal Station) Located outside Centraal Station.

I Amsterdam Visitor Centre Schiphol ◷7am-10pm) Inside Schiphol International Airport at the Arrivals 2 hall.

Travellers with Disabilities

➡ Travellers with reduced mobility will find Amsterdam moderately equipped to meet their needs.

➡ Most offices and museums have lifts and/

or ramps and toilets for visitors with disabilities.

➡ A large number of budget and midrange hotels have limited accessibility, as they occupy old buildings with steep stairs and no lifts.

➡ Restaurants tend to be on ground floors, though 'ground' sometimes includes a few steps.

➡ Most buses are wheelchair accessible, as are metro stations. Trams are becoming more accessible as new equipment is added. Many lines have elevated stops for wheelchair users. The GVB website (www.gvb.nl)

denotes which stops are wheelchair accessible.

➡ Accessible Travel Netherlands publishes a downloadable guide (www.accessibletravelnl. com/blogs/new-city-guide-for-Amsterdam) to restaurants, sights, transport and routes in Amsterdam for those with limited mobility.

➡ Check the accessibility guide at Accessible Amsterdam (www.toe gankelijkamsterdam.nl).

➡ Download Lonely Planet's free Accessible Travel guide from http:// lptravel.to/Accessible-Travel.

Dos & Don'ts

Greetings Do give a firm handshake and a double or triple cheek kiss.

Marijuana and Alcohol Don't smoke dope or drink beer on the streets.

Smoking Don't smoke (any substance) in bars or restaurants.

Bluntness Don't take offence if locals give you a frank, unvarnished opinion. It's not considered impolite, rather it comes from the desire to be direct and honest.

Cycling paths Don't walk in bike lanes (which are marked by white lines and bicycle symbols), and do look both ways before crossing a bike lane.

Visas

➡ Tourists from nearly 60 countries – including Australia, Canada, Israel, Japan, New Zealand, Singapore, South Korea, the USA and most of Europe – need only a valid passport to visit the Netherlands for up to three months.

➡ EU nationals can enter for three months with just their national identity card or a passport that expired less than five years ago.

➡ Nationals of most other countries need a Schengen visa, valid within the EU member states (except the UK and Ireland), plus Norway and Iceland, for 90 days within a six-month period.

➡ The Netherlands Foreign Affairs Ministry (www.government.nl) lists consulates and embassies around the world.

Language

The pronunciation of Dutch is fairly straightforward. If you read our coloured pronunciation guides as if they were English, you'll be understood just fine. Note that **öy** is pronounced as the 'er y' (without the 'r') in 'her year', and **kh** is a throaty sound, similar to the 'ch' in the Scottish *loch*. The stressed syllables are indicated with italics.

Where relevant, both polite and informal options in Dutch are included, indicated with 'pol' and 'inf' respectively.

To enhance your trip with a phrasebook, visit **lonelyplanet.com**. Lonely Planet iPhone phrasebooks are available through the Apple App store.

Basics

Hello.	*Dag./Hallo.*	dakh/ha·*loh*
Goodbye.	*Dag.*	dakh
Yes.	*Ja.*	yaa
No.	*Nee.*	ney

Please.
Alstublieft. (pol)		al·stew·*bleeft*
Alsjeblieft. (inf)		a·shuh·*bleeft*

Thank you.
Dank u/je. (pol/inf) dangk ew/yuh

Excuse me.
Excuseer mij. eks·kew·*zeyr* mey

How are you?
Hoe gaat het met u/jou? (pol/inf) hoo khaat huht met ew/yaw

Fine. And you?
Goed. En met u/jou? (pol/inf) khoot en met ew/yaw

Do you speak English?
Spreekt u Engels? spreykt ew *eng*·uhls

I don't understand.
Ik begrijp	ik buh·*khreyp*
het niet.	huht neet

Eating & Drinking

I'd like ...
Ik wil graag ... ik wil khraakh ...

a beer	*een bier*	uhn beer
a coffee	*een koffie*	uhn *ko*·fee
a table for two	*een tafel voor twee*	uhn *taa*·fuhl vohr twey
the menu	*een menu*	uhn me·*new*

I don't eat (meat).
Ik eet geen (vlees). ik eyt kheyn (vleys)

Delicious!
Heerlijk!/Lekker! *heyr*·luhk/*le*·kuhr

Cheers!
Proost! prohst

Please bring the bill.
Mag ik de	makh ik duh
rekening	*rey*·kuh·ning
alstublieft?	al·stew·*bleeft*

Shopping

I'd like to buy ...
Ik wil graag ...	ik wil khraakh ...
kopen.	*koh*·puhn

I'm just looking.
Ik kijk alleen maar. ik keyk a·*leyn* maar

How much is it?
Hoeveel kost het? hoo·*veyl* kost huht

That's too expensive.
Dat is te duur.   dat is tuh dewr

Can you lower the price?
Kunt u wat van de   kunt ew wat van duh
prijs afdoen?   preys af·doon

Emergencies

Help!
Help!   help

Call a doctor!
Bel een dokter!   bel uhn dok·tuhr

Call the police!
Bel de politie!   bel duh poh·leet·see

I'm sick.
Ik ben ziek.   ik ben zeek

I'm lost.
Ik ben verdwaald.   ik ben vuhr·dwaalt

Where are the toilets?
Waar zijn de   waar zeyn duh
toiletten?   twa·le·tuhn

Time & Numbers

What time is it?
Hoe laat is het?   hoo laat is huht

It's (10) o'clock.
Het is (tien) uur.   huht is (teen) ewr

Half past (10).
Half (elf).   half (elf)
(lit: half eleven)

morning	's ochtends	sokh·tuhns
afternoon	's middags	smi·dakhs
evening	's avonds	saa·vonts

yesterday	gisteren	khis·tuh·ruhn
today	vandaag	van·daakh
tomorrow	morgen	mor·khuhn

1	één	eyn
2	twee	twey
3	drie	dree
4	vier	veer
5	vijf	veyf
6	zes	zes
7	zeven	zey·vuhn
8	acht	akht
9	negen	ney·khuhn
10	tien	teen

Transport & Directions

Where's the ...?
Waar is ...?   waar is ...

How far is it?
Hoe ver is het?   hoo ver is huht

What's the address?
Wat is het adres?   wat is huht a·dres

Can you show me (on the map)?
Kunt u het mij   kunt ew huht mey
tonen (op de   toh·nuhn (op duh
kaart)?   kaart)

A ticket to ..., please.
Een kaartje naar   uhn kaar·chuh naar
..., graag.   ... khraakh

Please take me to ...
Breng me   breng muh
alstublieft   al·stew·bleeft
naar ...   naar ...

Does it stop at ...?
Stopt het in ...?   stopt huht in ...

I'd like to get off at ...
Ik wil graag in ...   ik wil khraak in ...
uitstappen.   öyt·sta·puhn

Can we get there by bike?
Kunnen we er   ku·nuhn wuh uhr
met de fiets heen?   met duh feets heyn

Behind the Scenes

Send Us Your Feedback

We love to hear from travellers – your comments help make our books better. We read every word, and we guarantee that your feedback goes straight to the authors. Visit **lonelyplanet.com/contact** to submit your updates and suggestions.

Note: We may edit, reproduce and incorporate your comments in Lonely Planet products such as guidebooks, websites and digital products, so let us know if you don't want your comments reproduced or your name acknowledged. For a copy of our privacy policy visit lonelyplanet.com/privacy.

Catherine's Thanks

Hartelijk bedankt first and foremost to Julian, and to everyone throughout Amsterdam and the Netherlands who provided insights, inspiration and good times during this update and over the years. Huge thanks too to Daniel Fahey and Abigail Blasi, and everyone at Lonely Planet. As ever, a heartfelt *merci encore* to my parents, brother, *belle-sœur* and *neveu*.

Abigail's Thanks

Huge thanks to Daniel Fahey for commissioning me, and Catherine Le Nevez for her support. A massive *dank je* to Jo Dufay for sharing her city knowledge and books, to Wouter Steenhuisen and Geerte Udo at iAmsterdam, to Esther Nelsey for local recommendations, and to Luca, Gabriel, Benjamin and Alessia for coming along for the ride.

Acknowledgements

Cover photograph: Keizersgracht and Leidsegracht canals, Jan Wlodarczyk/4Corners ©

This Book

This 5th edition of Lonely Planet's *Pocket Amsterdam* guidebook was curated by Catherine Le Nevez and researched and written by Catherine Le Nevez and Abigail Blasi. The previous edition was written by Karla Zimmerman. This guidebook was produced by the following:

Destination Editor
Daniel Fahey

Product Editors
Kate James, Grace Dobell

Senior Cartographer
Mark Griffiths

Cartographer
Anthony Phelan

Book Designer
Meri Blazevski

Assisting Editors Sarah Bailey, Judith Bamber, Victoria Harrison, Kristin Odijk, Tamara Sheward, Maja Vatrić

Cover Researcher
Naomi Parker

Thanks to Shona Gray, Noeleen Kestell, Claire Naylor, Karyn Noble, Lauren O'Connell, Rachel Rawling

Index

See also separate subindexes for:
Eating p188
Drinking p189
Entertainment p190
Shopping p190

Sights 000
Map Pages **000**

Our Writers

Catherine Le Nevez

Catherine's wanderlust kicked in when she road-tripped across Europe from her Parisian base aged four, and she's been hitting the road at every opportunity since, travelling to around 60 countries. Over the past dozen-plus years she's written scores of Lonely Planet guides and articles covering Paris, France, Europe and far beyond. Her work has also appeared in numerous online and print publications. Topping Catherine's list of travel tips is to travel without any expectations.

Abigail Blasi

A freelance travel writer, Abigail has lived and worked in London, Rome, Hong Kong and Copenhagen. Lonely Planet has sent her to India, Egypt, Tunisia, Mauritania, Mali, Italy, Portugal, Malta and around Britain. She writes regularly for newspapers and magazines including the *Independent*, the *Telegraph*, and *Lonely Planet Traveller*. She has three children and they often come along for the ride. She's @abiwhere on Twitter and Instagram.

Published by Lonely Planet Global Limited
CRN 554153
5th edition – May 2018
ISBN 978 1 78657 556 2
© Lonely Planet 2018   Photographs © as indicated 2018
10 9 8 7 6 5 4 3 2
Printed in Singapore

Although the authors and Lonely Planet have taken all reasonable care in preparing this book, we make no warranty about the accuracy or completeness of its content and, to the maximum extent permitted, disclaim all liability arising from its use.